SEW LUXE LEATHER

Over 20 Stylish Leather Craft Accessories

ROSANNA CLARE GETHIN

sewandso

www.sewandso.co.uk

CONTENTS

INTRODUCTION

I first became interested in working with leather whilst walking around Spitalfields Market in London. This was about 15 years ago and I'd just graduated from university with a degree in Graphic Design. Looking at the stalls of handmade goods, many by fashion graduates, I was especially drawn to the unique designs and the quality of the materials used, particularly the leather bags! However, as a recent graduate, I simply couldn't justify (or afford) to buy one; then I turned down the next aisle of stalls and came across a man selling hides of leather. There were all sorts of colours, textures, shapes and sizes, and I remember the overwhelming, amazing smell. Although I had never used a sewing machine, or worked with leather before, I decided there and then that I would have to learn. I bought two pieces of leather and asked my mum to teach me to sew. That was it – I was hooked!

I spent the next few years practising how to make leather bags and purses on my mother's little old Elna sewing machine with just a leather needle and standard sewing thread. It was a hobby that became more and more of a passion. Meanwhile, I had trained to be a Design Technology Teacher and brought some of the skills I had taught myself into the classroom. I introduced a bag making project to my GCSE classes and they loved it! After almost ten years teaching in schools, completing a Masters degree in Textile Design and taking several courses specifically in bag making, I decided to take the leap. I gave up my day job and started my own craft business making leather bags and accessories. However, I also used my teaching experience to run workshops and teach leather craft to adults both in groups and in one-to-one classes. That was three years ago now and it was the best decision I ever made. The classes are going from strength to strength and I feel that my teaching career gave me the crucial experience and confidence to teach leather craft.

The aim of the projects within this book is to teach you the basics of leatherwork, gradually allowing you to work up to more complex items. These projects are also designed so that you don't have to spend a fortune on tools and materials to get started. Like me, you can start with a small domestic sewing machine and a few affordable basics on the tiniest of budgets (so students and graduates rejoice!).

I hope you enjoy using this book as much as I did making it.

Happy sewing!

Rosanna x

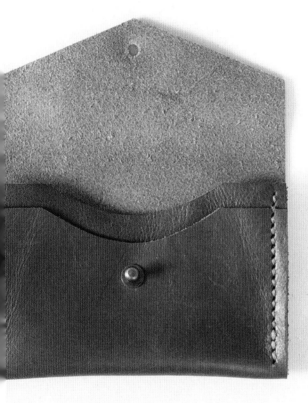

ALL ABOUT LEATHER

Leather is a durable, tactile and versatile material that has been used for countless products over thousands of years. In fact, it is one of a few materials that many believe actually improves with age! It is important to understand a bit about how leather is produced in order to best know how to choose, use and work with it. Leather comes from the skin of an animal, mainly cow, sheep and pig hide. The skin is treated to preserve it in a process known as tanning and there are two main methods of tanning leather: vegetable and chrome.

VEGETABLE TANNING

This is the traditional method utilising the tannins found in vegetable matter such as tree bark, wood, leaves and some fruits. Skins are soaked in liquid rich in these extracts, producing strong and firm leather. This type of leather is therefore perfect for making items like saddles, belts and shoes as it retains most of its natural oils making it easy to mould into shapes and emboss with pressure.

Traditionally, vegetable-tanned leather is perfect for a classic finish on favourite accessories.

CHROME TANNING (CHROME DYEING)

This is a relatively modern way of treating leather compared to vegetable tanning. Invented in the mid-19th century, it uses a solution of chemicals, acids and salts including chromium sulphate. This method creates softer, stretchier leather as the chemicals break down the natural fibres. It is a much faster method and the leather can be dyed in a wide variety of colours making it ideal for the fashion industry. However, it is considered more harmful to the environment due to the chemicals used. This may be something to consider when buying leather or deciding which projects to make. Due to its structure and softness, chrome-dyed leather generally requires heat for any embossing to be permanent.

Many leather suppliers have offcuts and sale pieces of vegetable-tanned and chrome-dyed leather large enough for many projects in this book.

Chrome-dyed leather allows for a variety of colours to be incorporated into your projects.

VEGETABLE VS. CHROME

Generally, vegetable-tanned leather is better for hand stitching and chrome-dyed leather is better for machine sewing. If in doubt, ask when you buy and explain what you wish to make with it; the supplier will advise you as to which is the most suitable leather to buy.

BUYING LEATHER

When starting out with leatherwork it is advisable to purchase your leather in person, allowing you to handle and check it for any holes or imperfections. Leather can be very expensive and usually the smallest quantity you can buy is half a hide which, depending on the thickness and quality, could cost £30 to £300! Hides or large pieces are usually sold by size (square footage) and graded by thickness; offcuts are priced by weight. Start with small projects that allow you to buy offcuts or reduced leather from sale bins. Then work up to buying larger pieces when you are more confident in your skills, have more understanding of how leather works when sewing, and know the colours and types with which you like working. Unless you need to create many pieces in the same leather on a regular basis, you may never need to buy a full hide.

FULL GRAIN VS. TOP GRAIN

With the actual grain of the leather, you will find two options:
Full grain leather retains the natural grain on the surface, meaning it will develop a natural patina over time. It retains strength and durability but is more susceptible to stains and marks.
Top grain leather has had its top layer sanded away to remove the natural grain and top fibres, reducing its strength. An imitation grain is sometimes applied for a more uniform look. A surface finish or coating is often applied making the leather more stain-resistant.

GLOSSARY

Use this quick reference to help you become familiar with the leather-craft terms used in the book.

AWL

A small metal pointed tool used for piercing holes, especially in leather

BAGGING OUT

Turning a bag or purse the right way around after sewing inside out

BEESWAX

Used to coat linen thread for hand stitching or edges of leather before burnishing

BURNISHING

Polishing leather by rubbing with a rounded tool or cloth (only used on vegetable-tanned leather)

CHROME DYEING

The method of tanning leather using chromium, usually used for lighter weight skins

CREASE

The mark or channel made in leather to help create an accurate fold

EMBOSSING

A way of creating patterns in leather, usually lettering or pre-made stamp designs

GRAIN

The natural texture of the leather's surface if it hasn't been altered

GUSSET

A piece of material sewn into a bag or purse to enlarge or to give more depth

HIDE

A full skin of animal leather, usually the largest size you can get

LACING PONY OR CLAMP

Used to hold your work so that both hands are free when hand stitching

NAPPA

A piece of full grain sheep skin

PARING (SKIVING)

Thinning or shaving the underside of leather to remove bulk for folding or layering (usually done around the edge or on corners only)

PRESS FASTENER

A fastening that consists of two pairs of components – male and female. A great fastening for many leather projects

PRICKING IRON (STITCHING FORK)

A tool with diamond shaped prongs to make holes for hand stitching. Usually comes with between one and six prongs, with different widths between each

PUNCH

A metal tool used to make holes; comes in different sizes and can be a single punch or rotary hole puncher

RIVET (DOUBLE CAPPED)

A permanent fastening that consists of two parts that clip together to create a strong join when pressed with a special tool. Comes in different finishes, cap sizes and shaft lengths

ROTARY HOLE PUNCHER

Tool with various sized punches to make holes, often used for belts

SAM BROWNE STUD

A stud-and-screw fastening used with thicker or vegetable-tanned leathers, and named after the man who invented it!

SCORING

Marking the leather with a thin scratch line that acts as a guide for punching holes

VEGETABLE TANNING

A method of preserving leather using vegetable matter such as bark and sumac

TOOL BOX

As with any craft, the number and variety of tools required can be vast and never-ending, not to mention expensive. However, there are just a few essential tools required with leatherwork to get you started. Once you have decided that you love your new hobby (and you will, trust me!), you can start adding to it gradually and affordably (*see* Resources).

GENERAL CRAFT TOOLS

You may already have many of these tools as part of other crafts or DIY.

CUTTING MAT

A large A3 mat will allow you to cut longer lengths of leather in one easy movement and provides plenty of working space in general. A smaller A4 mat is useful if you are short of space or to use for smaller pieces of work (a).

METAL RULERS

You should have one flat ruler for quick and easy measurements, and a safety ruler for using with blades and cutters, if you prefer (b).

TAPE MEASURE

Bag straps and belts tend to be fairly long, so a tape measure may be needed for easy measuring (c).

SCALPEL

I use a grade 3 Swann Morten handle with 10a blades for safe and accurate cutting (d).

ROTARY CUTTER

OLFA is a good brand. I recommend using the medium sized 45mm diameter handle and blades (e).

BULLDOG CLIPS

Leather can't be pinned as the holes will be permanent, so bulldog clips are ideal for securing layers of leather while glue dries, or as you sew (f).

MASKING TAPE

Use masking tape to secure layers of leather as you work, or to mask off areas for decorative cutting (g).

PLIERS

Pliers are handy for manipulating the hardware used for bags such as D-rings and zippers (h).

SCISSORS

Keep a pair of fabric scissors for cutting bag linings and other fabrics only, then another general craft pair for cutting card, paper, tape, and so on (i).

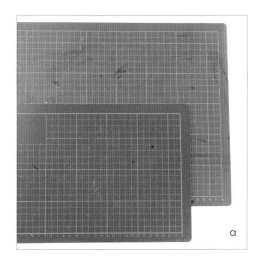

a

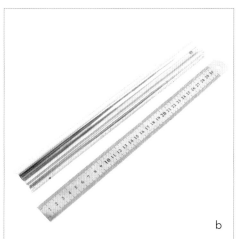

b

c

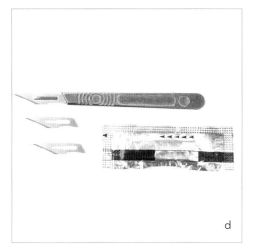

d

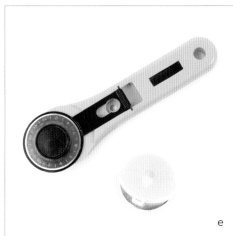

e

f

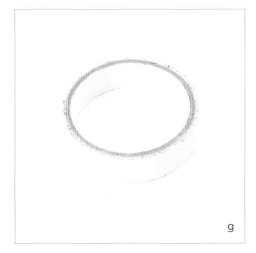

g

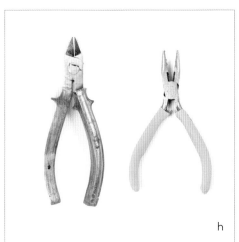

h

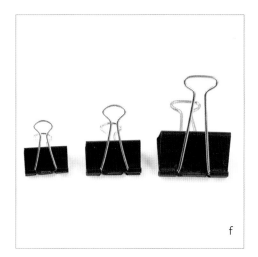

i

BASIC LEATHER CRAFT TOOLS

These are the basic tools you will find yourself using time and time again throughout this book.

LEATHER MARKER PEN

Pins, ordinary ink and other marking tools can leave permanent blemishes on the leather. A special pen for marking leather leaves a visible mark on the grain, but rubs away easily when no longer needed (a).

PRICKING IRON

Available in various sizes (e.g. 4, 5 and 6mm width prongs), this is an essential tool for creating accurate, straight lines of holes in leather for hand stitching (b).

ROTARY HOLE PUNCHER

Brands such as Drapers make excellent hole punching tools. A rotary (revolving) tool includes several sizes of punch on a single tool, from 2–4.5mm ($\frac{1}{8}$–$\frac{1}{4}$in) in diameter. Invest in a good quality one as cheap ones buckle fairly swiftly (c).

SINGLE HOLE PUNCHING TOOL

To punch a hole further in from the leather's edge than the rotary puncher will reach, a hollow punch set is useful (d).

RUBBER HEADED MALLET

Use with hole-making tools, such as the pricking iron, to safely apply the force needed to punch through even thicker leather (e).

NYLON PLASTIC MAT

This will protect your work surface from hole punching tools that require a mallet. A plastic kitchen chopping board is perfect for this.

AWL

As well as being useful for marking lines on the leather, an awl also helps to open up holes made with the pricking iron to make hand stitching easier (f).

LEATHER NEEDLES

Sewing needles made specifically for hand stitching leather are ideal for using with waxed thread, as are large embroidery needles. The needle can have either a sharp or blunt tip – if you have punched your holes well it won't matter which you use. I prefer sharp tips as they move through the leather more easily (g).

WAXED THREAD

Use nylon or waxed linen thread for hand stitching leather. This thread is designed to be extra strong, and the waxing allows the thread to glide smoothly through the holes as you stitch.

CONTACT ADHESIVE

A medium strength latex glue, such as Copydex, is solvent-free and ideal for securing layers of leather before sewing.

IMPACT ADHESIVE

Stronger than Copydex, this glue is used in shoe manufacture and bag making, and can be bought in a tin called Evo-Stik Impact Adhesive. It has a strong smell and must be used in a well ventilated area.

SANDPAPER

When applying glue to the smooth side of leather, you have to create a 'key' using fairly coarse sandpaper first. About P60 to P80 grit is best.

BEESWAX AND BURNISHER

Rub beeswax and a burnisher on the edges of your projects to create a smooth and durable finish (h).

SADDLE SOAP

Clean, condition and protect your leather creations using saddle soap. Used on vegetable-tanned leather only (i).

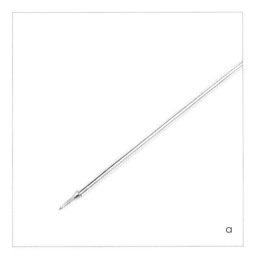

a

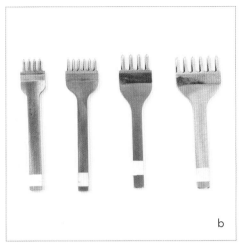

b

c

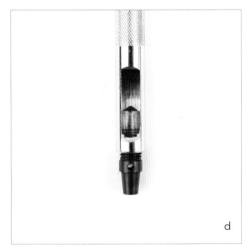

d

e

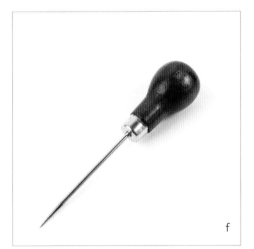

f

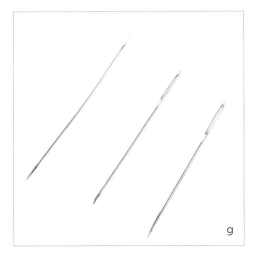

g

h

i

SPECIALIST LEATHER CRAFT TOOLS

After you gain more experience and discover what you enjoy creating from leather, you might be interested in investing in more specialist tools.

LACING PONY

This simple but useful tool is a leather-friendly 'vice' to hold your project, leaving you with both hands free for hand stitching (a). The one shown is my own design; commercial versions have a screw for tightening. An alternative is to hold the project between your knees.

STRAP CUTTER

This allows you to cut long, even and continuous strips of leather with ease, ideal for bag straps and belts (b).

BELT-END CUTTER

Usually available in sets including different sizes, this cutter is used with a mallet to give an instant rounded end to straps and belts (c).

CLICKER KNIFE

With a handle and interchangeable blades, this knife is similar to a scalpel but is more heavy-duty and made especially for leatherwork.

TABLE MOUNTED RIVET TOOL

Rivets can be set into leather with a hand tool and mallet. However, a table mounted version allows it to be done with much more ease, speed and accuracy (d).

EDGE PAINT/DYE

The edges of leather can be painted with a specialist paint or dye to add colour, perfect for a professional finish and for adding a pop of colour (e).

EMBOSSING LETTER SET

Emboss initials, names, numbers and even logos into leather using an embossing set. This technique is most effective on thicker vegetable-tanned leather (f).

HOT FOILING MACHINE

For a luxe finish, hot foiling adds metallic detail. The machine needed is an investment, so more suitable for anyone taking up leather craft professionally.

METAL HARDWARE

Metal fittings such as press fasteners (g), zippers, Sam Browne studs and buckles come in a variety of finishes and sizes (*see* Resources). You can buy many items online but beware of 'cheap' versions as the quality is often compromised and they can be faulty or break easily. *See* Techniques: Inserting Fastenings for more details and how to fit them.

SEWING MACHINE

For the machine sewn projects in this book, a home sewing machine (h) is suitable with only a couple of special additions:

LEATHER MACHINE NEEDLES

To help cut a hole through the leather, these needles are spear shaped to cut as the stitch is being formed. Using the correct needle will give better results and keep your sewing machine in good shape.

WALKING FOOT

With thick items that need more of a 'push' through the sewing machine, a walking foot is invaluable. The foot eases the leather over the footplate from the top, in the same way as your machine's feed dogs do from beneath (i).

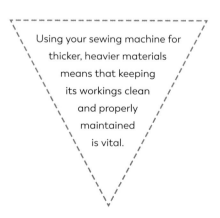

Using your sewing machine for thicker, heavier materials means that keeping its workings clean and properly maintained is vital.

a

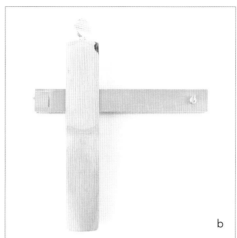

b

c

d

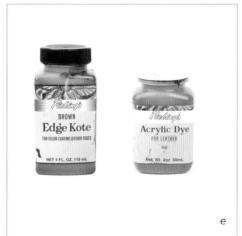

e

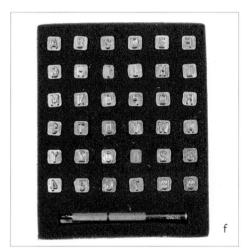

f

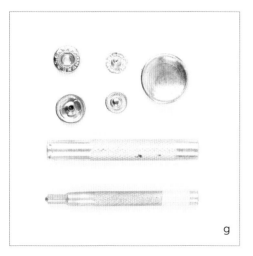

g

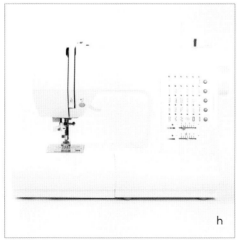

h

i

TASSEL KEYRING

This is the perfect accessory for any handbag or set of keys that need a bit of colour. It's also a great project on which to practise your cutting and gluing skills – and there's no sewing required.

 No sew

 16 x 14cm (6¼ x 5½in) piece of chrome-dyed leather, 1–1.4mm thick

You will need:

· 30mm (1⅛in) lobster clasp

Finished size:

15 x 2.5cm (5⅞ x 1in)

1. Cut out as follows:

• One rectangle of leather 14 x 12cm (5$\frac{1}{2}$ x 4$\frac{3}{4}$in) for the tassel

• One rectangle of leather 6 x 1cm (2$\frac{3}{8}$ x $\frac{3}{8}$in) for the tab

2. Feed the tab piece through the clasp ring and apply glue to the *wrong side* of the leather on either end. Leave to dry for a few minutes before sticking the ends together (a).

3. Place the tassel piece *right side up* on your cutting mat and secure the top of the tassel – one of the 14cm (5$\frac{1}{2}$in) edges – to the mat with masking tape. Ensure that the lower edge of the masking tape is 2cm ($\frac{3}{4}$in) from the top edge of the tassel piece.

4. Cut straight lines from the lower edge of the masking tape down to the bottom of the tassel piece in approximately 5mm ($\frac{1}{4}$in) intervals (b).

5. On the *right side* of the leather, sand and apply glue to the left half of the uncut section of the tassel piece – *see Techniques: Gluing* (c). You might need to use impact adhesive to achieve a firm enough bond, rather than contact adhesive, depending on your leather. Test the glue on a sample of leather first.

6. Turn the tassel piece over and apply glue to the uncut section on the *wrong side* of the leather. Apply a small amount of glue to the bottom of the tab (as this is the *right side* of the leather you may need to rub this with sandpaper first to help the glue stick). Place the tab onto the edge of the glued section on the *wrong side* of the tassel piece (d).

7. Once the glue is tacky, tightly roll the tab inside the tassel, keeping the edges even as you roll (e). Place a clamp or bulldog clip around the top of the tassel while it dries. Leave for at least 1 hour before releasing.

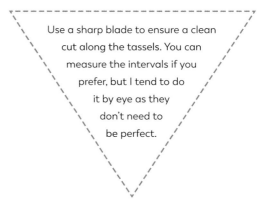

Use a sharp blade to ensure a clean cut along the tassels. You can measure the intervals if you prefer, but I tend to do it by eye as they don't need to be perfect.

a

b

c

d

e

This tassel keyring is the perfect project for complete beginners, as it's quick to make and doesn't require any special tools.

FRINGED BOOKMARK

This is a great taster project to get you started with the basics of marking and cutting out leather. Why not make a few as gifts for friends and family – everyone needs a bookmark!

 No sew

 20 x 6cm (7⁷⁄₈ x 2³⁄₈in) piece of vegetable-tanned or chrome-dyed leather, 1.2–2mm thick

Finished size:
18 x 4cm (7¹⁄₈ x 1⁵⁄₈in)

1. Cut out the bookmark templates (*see* Templates) from thick card and transfer all markings onto the card.

2. Use these templates to cut out the main body and tassel from the leather (**a**). *See* Techniques: Cutting.

3. Place masking tape 4cm (1⅝in) from the bottom edge of the bookmark. Using the template as a guide, mark the intervals that will form the tasselled end along the tape's edge (**b**).

4. Position the tip of the scalpel at the edge of the masking tape and cut the fringe, using the marks and ruler as a guide (**c**).

5. Using the template again as a guide, punch a 4mm (⅛in) hole at the top of the bookmark (**d**).

6. Take the skinny length of leather and fold in half, *wrong sides together*, to form a loop. Thread the loop through the hole you've just made (**e**).

7. Thread the ends through the loop and gently pull taut to form the tassel (**f**).

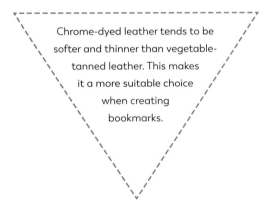

Chrome-dyed leather tends to be softer and thinner than vegetable-tanned leather. This makes it a more suitable choice when creating bookmarks.

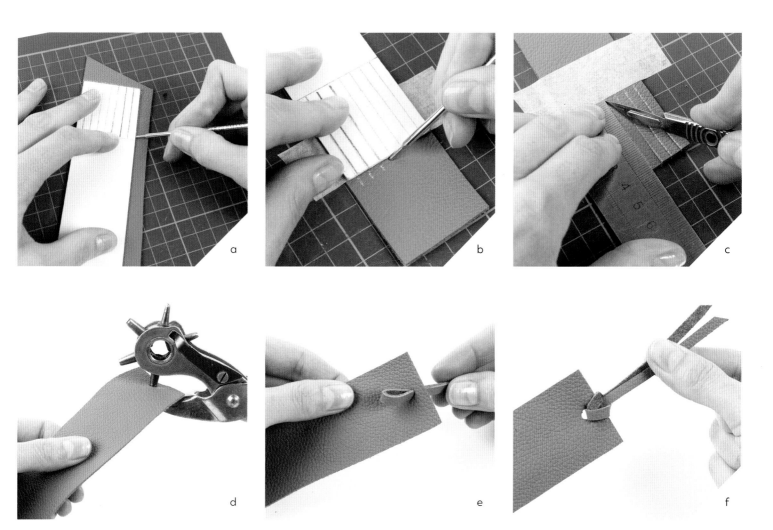

BOLD CUFFS

These versatile cuffs in two styles are simple to make; comfortable due to being made from softer chrome-dyed leather, they are totally on trend. You'll be the envy of your friends, so prepare to take orders!

 No sew

 Option 1:
30 x 7cm (11³/₄ x 2³/₄in) piece of vegetable-tanned or chrome-dyed leather, 1.2–2mm thick

Option 2:
30 x 5cm (11³/₄ x 2in) piece of vegetable-tanned or chrome-dyed leather, 1.2–2mm thick

You will need:
- Option 1: Sam Browne stud 5mm (¹/₄in)
- Option 2: Press fastener 10–15mm (³/₈–⁵/₈in)

Finished size:
Option 1: To fit wrist x 5cm (2in)
Option 2: To fit wrist x 2cm (³/₄in)

OPTION 1

SLICED CUFF

1. First, measure the circumference of your wrist and add 2cm ($^3/_4$in) to allow for a 1cm ($^3/_8$in) overlap on each end. Use this length to adjust the template if need be (*see* Templates) (a). Use the template to cut out the main shape of the cuff using a ruler and rotary cutter or scalpel. Transfer all markings onto the leather with a pencil.

2. Place masking tape 2cm ($^3/_4$in) from the top and bottom edges. Follow the marks you made to cut nine slices each 5mm ($^1/_4$in) apart between the strips of tape (b).

3. Punch out the top hole 1cm ($^3/_8$in) from the end, as marked on the template (c).

4. Place the Sam Browne stud through the hole and tighten up (*see* Techniques: Inserting Fastenings) (d).

5. Cross-cut the opposite end of the cuff 1cm ($^3/_8$in) in from the end (e). The cuts should be no more than 1cm ($^3/_8$in) each way depending on the thickness of leather and size of stud. The thicker the leather, the longer the cuts may need to be. Test on a piece of scrap leather first.

6. Push the stud through to join the two ends together (f).

OPTION 2

PUNCHED CUFF

1. Measure your wrist and adjust the template as described in Step 1 of the Sliced Cuff. Use a hole punching tool to position and cut the holes on the template (g). Mark out the leather using the template and cut out using a ruler and rotary cutter or scalpel. Transfer markings onto the leather with a pencil.

2. Round off the ends of the cuff with a belt-end cutter and mallet, or cut carefully with a sharp scalpel (*see* Techniques: Rounding Off Ends).

3. Mark holes on the leather using the template and punch out carefully (h).

4. Punch out the top and bottom hole of the cuff and add the press fastener to each end (*see* Techniques: Inserting Fastenings).

To help you get the correct fit, make a paper version of the cuff first and use this to adjust to the template.

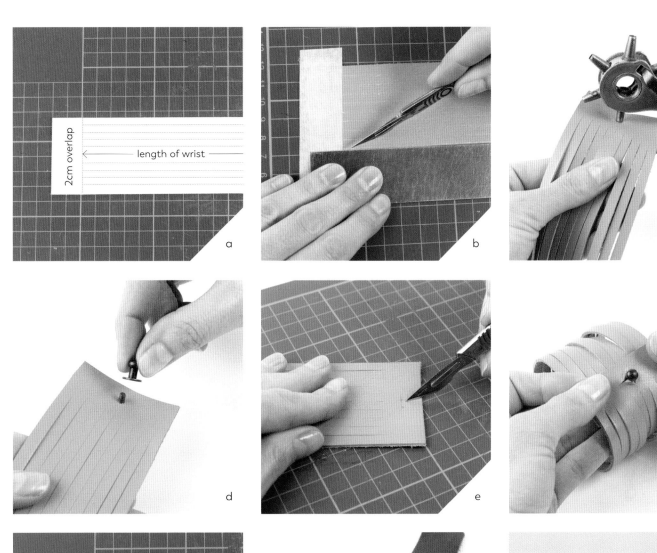

2cm overlap

← length of wrist →

a

b

c

d

e

f

overlap ← width of wrist →

g

h

Remember, the template markings
and measurements are a guide.
Change them according to your own
tastes for a truly unique accessory.

CARD HOLDER

Get to grips with the basics of stitching leather by hand with this simple card holder project. Using traditional saddlery techniques, the stitching adds detail to an otherwise minimalist design.

Hand stitched

22 x 10cm (8⅝ x 4in) piece of vegetable-tanned or smooth chrome-dyed leather, 1.2–2mm thick maximum

You will need:

• Pricking iron 4mm (⅛in) spacing

Finished size:

8 x 10cm (3⅛ x 4in)

1. Cut out:

- One rectangle of leather 20 x 8cm (7⅞ x 3⅛in). This size allows around three credit cards and a note or two.

2. Apply a thin layer of glue about 5mm (¼in) wide along each long edge on the *wrong side* of the leather. Allow the glue to go tacky (**a**).

3. Fold the leather in half as carefully as possible, making sure the edges are evenly matched, then press together all the way to the fold (**b**). Trim off any uneven edges with a ruler and sharp scalpel.

4. Using an awl and ruler, score a line 5mm (¼in) in from the edge along each side to be stitched (*see* Techniques: Scoring & Punching). This will be your guideline for punching the holes.

5. Starting at the cut edge, place the pricking iron along the guideline with the first prong sitting just over the edge (**c**). Make sure you have a thick piece of scrap leather underneath to help the hole punch to go through the leather, and hit with a mallet. Use the last hole from the first set as the first hole for the second set of holes and so on. Stop when you are approximately 5–10mm (¼–⅜in) from the fold (this distance will depend on the thickness of the leather; avoid punching in the fold itself).

6. Push the awl through all of the holes by about 2cm (¾in) to make them bigger, as this will ease the sewing process (*see* Techniques: Scoring & Punching).

7. Cut a piece of your chosen thread four times longer than the area to be stitched and thread a needle onto each end, pulling the thread through by approximately 10cm (4in) (*see* Techniques: Hand Stitching). Set up the lacing pony – if you don't have one, just hold the case between your knees.

8. Complete your stitching on both sides of the case (**d**), cut the threads and burn the ends.

9. Cut out a scoop (optional) using a 2cm (¾in) belt-end cutter or scalpel (*see* Techniques: Cutting) (**e**).

10. If you have used vegetable-tanned leather, finish by rubbing in a layer of saddle soap with a cloth. This helps protect the leather from marks and stains (important for frequently handled items). *See* Techniques: Surface Treatments.

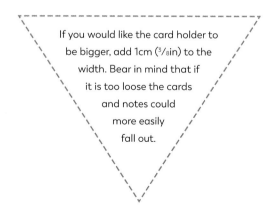

If you would like the card holder to be bigger, add 1cm (⅜in) to the width. Bear in mind that if it is too loose the cards and notes could more easily fall out.

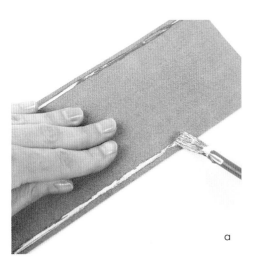

a

b

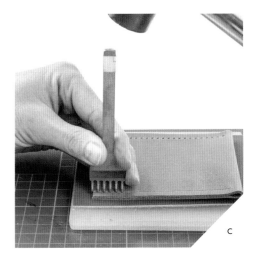

c

d

e

Keep the two lines of glue 2–3mm
(¹⁄₈in) in from the edge of the
leather to avoid it squeezing
out of the sides when folded.

LUGGAGE TAG

Make your luggage stand out from the crowd with a personalised tag. The practical additions of bold metal hardware and an optional acetate window ensure a professional looking finish.

 Hand stitched

 20 x 25cm (7⁷⁄₈ x 9⁷⁄₈in) piece of vegetable-tanned or smooth chrome-dyed leather, 1.8–2mm thick

NB if you want to use contrasting colours as shown, ensure you have enough of each colour before cutting out

You will need:

· Clear acetate 6 x 8cm (2³⁄₈ x 3¹⁄₈in) (optional)
· Pricking iron 4mm (¹⁄₈in) spacing
· Press fastener 15mm (⁵⁄₈in)
· Rivet 6mm (¹⁄₄in)

Finished size:
13 x 7.5cm (5¹⁄₈ x 3in)

1. Mark out the front and back (main body) pieces and strap of the luggage tag using the templates (*see* Templates) (**a**). Mark the holes then cut out the pieces with a rotary cutter or scalpel and punch the holes. Don't forget to cut the window from the *front piece only*.

2. If you wish to add the acetate window, use the template to cut the acetate to size, then apply a thin layer of impact adhesive up to 5mm (¼in) in from the edge all around the edge of the *right side* of the acetate window (**b**). Repeat around the *wrong side* of the window in the leather, leave to go tacky, and press the pieces together.

3. Attach the male part of the press fastener to the front piece (**c**) (*see* Techniques: Inserting Fastenings), then apply glue around the edge of the *wrong side* of each main body piece and press together. Add the female part of the press fastener to the strap as shown (**d**).

4. Use a ruler and awl to score a border 5mm (¼in) in from the edge all around the front of the tag (*see* Techniques: Scoring & Punching). Next, punch holes along the line using the pricking iron and mallet making sure the prongs of the pricking iron have gone all the way through the leather (**e**).

5. Push the awl through the holes to open them up a bit to make stitching easier (**f**).

6. Cut a piece of your chosen thread four times longer than the area to be stitched and thread a needle onto each end, pulling the thread through by approximately 10cm (4in). Set up your lacing pony and clamp your piece in place with the top side on the left as shown (**g**) and saddle stitch (*see* Techniques: Hand Stitching).

7. Punch the hole for the strap (**h**), then rivet in place (**i**). *See* Techniques: Inserting Fastenings.

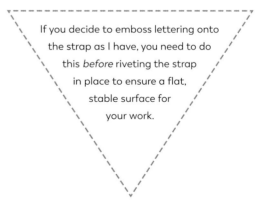

If you decide to emboss lettering onto the strap as I have, you need to do this *before* riveting the strap in place to ensure a flat, stable surface for your work.

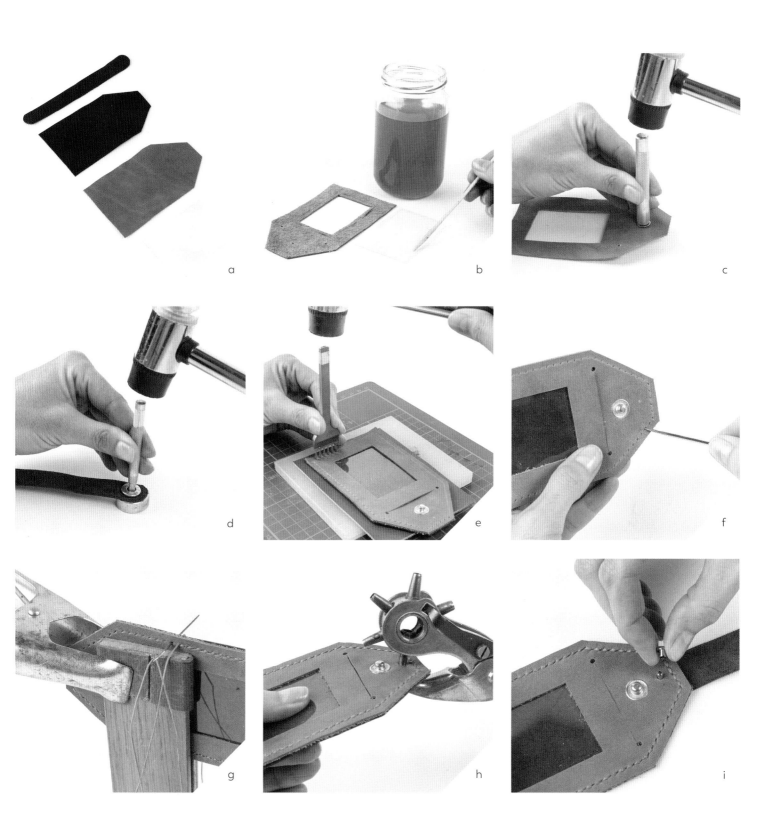

a

b

c

d

e

f

g

h

i

EARPHONE HOLDERS

These holders are the perfect storage for your earphones, keeping them safe and tangle free. In addition, they'll get you started with the basics of cutting, gluing and machine-sewing leather.

 Options 1 and 2: No sew

 Option 3: Machine sewn

 Options 1 and 2:
12 x 12cm (4³/₄ x 4³/₄in) piece of vegetable-tanned leather, 1.4–2.5mm thick

Option 3:
12 x 12cm (4³/₄ x 4³/₄in) piece of chrome-dyed leather, 1–1.4mm thick

You will need:

• Options 1 and 2: Sam Browne stud 5mm (¹/₄in)

• Option 3: Press fastener 10–15mm (³/₈–⁵/₈in)

Finished size:

Options 1 and 2: 10 x 5cm (4 x 2in)
Option 3: 10 x 7cm (4 x 2³/₄in)

OPTION 1

SNAP AND GO

1. Copy the template for Option 1 (*see* Templates) onto the *wrong side* of the leather with a leather marker pen and cut out. Mark and punch the holes (**a**).

2. Add the Sam Browne stud (*see* Techniques: Inserting Fastenings) (**b**).

OPTION 2

CLEVER CUT OUTS

1. Copy the template for Option 2 (*see* Templates) onto the *wrong side* of the leather with a leather marker pen and cut out. Mark and punch the holes.

2. Mark the notches from the template onto both sides of the circle (**c**), and cut with a sharp scalpel. These grooves help to keep the earphone lead in place.

3. Add the Sam Browne stud (*see* Techniques: Inserting Fastenings).

OPTION 3

SAFE AND SOUND

1. Copy both parts of the template (*see* Templates) onto the *wrong side* of the leather with a leather marker pen, then cut out.

2. Apply glue (*see* Techniques: Gluing) around the bottom curved edge of both pieces (**d**) and press together when tacky.

3. Use a sewing machine to stitch the glued edge, remembering to reverse stitch at each end (**e**). *See* Techniques: Machine Sewing.

4. Mark the hole from the template on the full circle only and punch out. Place the earphones inside the pouch and fold the flap over. Use the existing hole to mark the position for the second hole and punch out (**f**).

5. Add the female part of the press fastener to the front of the case (**g**), and the male part to the flap (**h**). *See* Techniques: Inserting Fastenings.

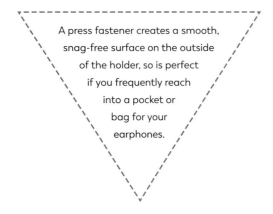

A press fastener creates a smooth, snag-free surface on the outside of the holder, so is perfect if you frequently reach into a pocket or bag for your earphones.

a

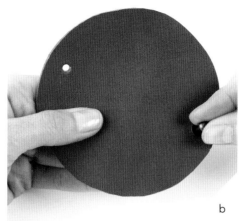

b

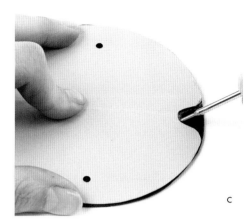

c

d

e

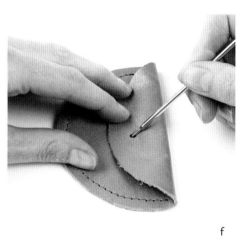

f

g

h

Combine your own choice of coloured leather, thread shade and fastening to create customised results.

GLASSES CASE

This project uses thicker, more rigid leather to create a gently curved case in which to safely store your reading glasses. Make a case for your sunglasses too – they'll thank you for it!

 Hand stitched

 20 x 20cm (7⅞ x 7⅞in) piece of vegetable-tanned leather, 2–3mm thick

You will need:

• Pricking iron 6mm (¼in) spacing

Finished size:

18 x 9cm (7⅞ x 3½in) or adjust size to fit glasses

1. Cut out (a):

• One square of leather 18 x 18cm (7¹/₈ x 7¹/₈in), or adjust size to fit glasses. Make a curved guide using strong card and the corner template (*see* Templates). Use this template to cut the rounded corners (*see* Techniques: Rounding Off Ends).

2. Decide which side of the case will be the opening. Apply contact adhesive around the *wrong side* of the other three sides of the leather, then carefully press these sides together and secure with bulldog clips (b).

3. Starting 3cm (1¹/₈in) down from the opening, use a ruler and awl to score a border 5mm (¹/₄in) in from the edge all around the two front edges of the case to be stitched (c).

4. Punch the holes along the line using the pricking iron and mallet, making sure the prongs have gone all the way through the leather. Gently rock the iron forward and back to pull out the prongs (*see* Techniques: Scoring & Punching). Push the awl through the holes to open them up a little to make stitching easier (d).

5. Cut a piece of your chosen thread four times longer than the area to be stitched (*see* Techniques: Hand Stitching) and thread a needle onto each end pulling the thread through by approximately 10cm (4in) (e).

6. Set up your lacing pony and clamp the case in place with top side on the left. Saddle stitch along the sides (f), then trim and burn the ends of the thread (g).

7. Rub beeswax along the edge of the case and polish with a burnisher until the edge is smooth and rounded (*see* Techniques: Surface Treatments) (h).

a

b

c

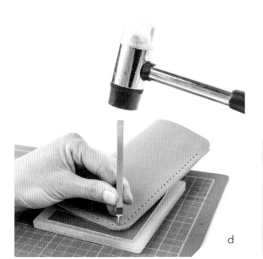

d

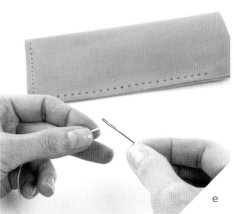

e

f

g

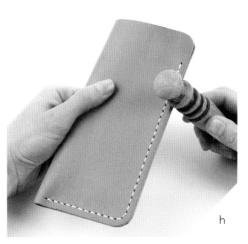

h

If you wish to emboss lettering
onto the case, do so after cutting
out the leather, but before
you glue down the sides.

PASSPORT HOLDER

A must-have addition to your travel wardrobe, this cover will help protect your passport and keep your documents safe when you go away. Contrasting coloured thread adds interest to a simple shape.

  Hand stitched

  35 x 25cm (13³/₄ x 9⁷/₈in) piece of vegetable-tanned leather, 1.2–2mm thick

You will need:

· Pricking iron 6mm (¹/₄in) spacing

Finished size:

15 x 10.5cm (5⁷/₈ x 4¹/₈in)

1. Cut out as follows (**a**):
- Two rectangles of leather each 15 x 21cm (5$^7/_8$ x 8$^1/_4$in).
- Cut *one* of these pieces into three smaller rectangles: two rectangles 6 x 15cm (2$^3/_8$ x 5$^7/_8$in) each, and one rectangle 9 x 15cm (3$^1/_2$ x 5$^7/_8$in)

2. Lay one of the 6 x 15cm (2$^3/_8$ x 5$^7/_8$in) pieces on top of the 9 x 15cm (3$^1/_2$ x 5$^7/_8$in) piece, *right side* up. I ine up the two longer edges and mark where the smaller piece ends on the larger piece. Scratch away the edge of the leather on the larger piece to create a 'key', staying within the area covered by the smaller piece (**b**). *See* Techniques: Gluing.

3. On the *wrong side*, apply glue to the two short sides and one long side of the 6 x 15cm (2$^3/_8$ x 5$^7/_8$in) piece. On the *right side* apply glue to the scratched area of the 9 x 15cm (3$^1/_2$ x 5$^7/_8$in) piece (**c**). Allow to go tacky, then press together.

4. Measure the long side of the top piece of leather to find the centre (**d**). Mark five stitches in from the open edge for stitching.

5. With the pricking iron, punch six holes through both layers of leather and saddle stitch (**e**). As this is a short section, you can reverse all the way back to the beginning (rather than just two stitches) for a more even looking finish.

6. On the *wrong side*, glue along the three edges to be stitched on both end-pieces of leather. Do the same on corresponding edges of the 15 x 21cm (5$^7/_8$ x 8$^1/_4$in) cover piece (**f**). Allow to dry, then press together (**g**).

7. On the outside of the cover, mark a guideline using the awl and ruler 5mm (¼in) from the edge. Punch holes using a 6mm (¼in) pricking iron (*see* Techniques: Scoring & Punching) (**h**).

8. Saddle stitch all the way round (*see* Techniques: Hand Stitching). You will need a very long piece of thread – approximately 270cm (106¼in) – so it may be awkward to sew until you have covered the first half. The alternative is to complete the stitching in two halves, with a join halfway along. If you do sew it in two halves, make sure the threads are joined on the back or on a corner to help disguise it.

9. Use a sharp scalpel to trim away the tip of the corners. Be careful to keep the blade away from the stitching, cutting no closer than 2mm (⅛in) away from the stitched line (**i**).

10. Finish off the edges by burnishing them if you so wish (*see* Techniques: Surface Treatments).

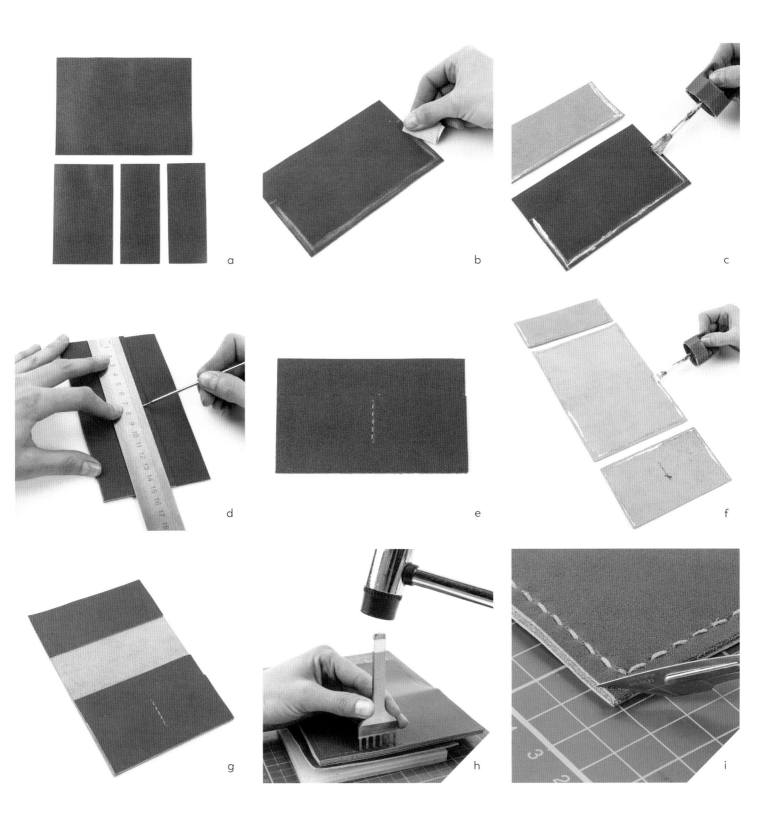

a

b

c

d

e

f

g

h

i

ZIPPER PURSE

This purse has endless uses: it can hold travel money, a few cards, or essential make-up on a night out. Whatever the purpose, it makes a great addition to any wardrobe. It's also a chance to get your teeth into machine sewing leather and inserting a zipper.

 Machine sewn

 20 x 32cm (7⁷/₈ x 12⁵/₈in) piece of chrome-dyed leather, 1–1.4mm thick

6 x 10cm (2³/₈ x 4in) piece of metallic leather, 0.8–1.4mm thick for triangle design

You will need:

· Lining fabric (cotton or poly-cotton) 20 x 32cm (7⁷/₈ x 12⁵/₈in)

· Metal zipper 12.7cm (5in)

· Rivet 6mm (¹/₄in) for zipper pull (optional)

Finished size:

14 x 11.5cm (5¹/₂ x 4¹/₂in)

1. Cut out as follows:

- Two rectangles of chrome-dyed leather each 17 x 14cm (6³/₄ x 5¹/₂in)
- One strip of chrome-dyed leather 10 x 1cm (4 x ³/₈in) for zipper pull (optional)
- One triangle of metallic leather (*see* Templates)
- Two rectangles of lining fabric each 17 x 14cm (6³/₄ x 5¹/₂in)

2. Trim a 1 x 1cm (³/₈ x ³/₈in) triangle from the two top corners on each rectangle of leather with a scalpel. Apply contact adhesive in a 2cm (³/₄in) wide strip along the top edge on the *wrong side*. Leave for approximately 10 minutes until it is tacky and has turned clear. Then carefully fold the glued section in half along the edge, keeping it even all the way along (**a**).

3. Apply glue to the *wrong side* of the triangle piece and to a small area in the centre of the *right side* of one of the leather rectangles. When the glue is tacky, press the glued sides together, ensuring that the triangle's point is centred along the width of the rectangle. The triangle itself should be positioned slightly higher – approximately 3cm (1¹/₈in) – to allow for the seam allowance at the bottom. Set up your sewing machine (*see* Techniques: Machine Sewing) with cream or gold thread and sew in place (**b**).

4. Attach a zipper foot to your sewing machine. Apply glue to the ends of the zipper on the back and fold each side outwards. Align the zipper with the top edge of the lining fabric (on the fabric's *right side*) with the zipper pull on the right. Sew the edge of the zipper along the edge of the lining fabric (**c**). *See* Techniques: Inserting a Zipper for more tips.

5. Place the *wrong side* of the folded edge of the leather back piece on top of the stitched zipper, securing with masking tape underneath to hold in place. Sew along 5mm (¹/₄in) from the edge of the leather ensuring that the stitch line remains parallel with the zipper teeth (**d**). Once sewn, pull the back lining fabric to lie flat underneath the back leather, *wrong sides together*.

6. Position the second edge of the zipper on the top edge of the *right side* of the front lining piece and sew together as before (**e**).

7. Place the *wrong side* of the folded edge of the leather back piece on top of the stitched zipper, securing with masking tape underneath. Sew along 5mm (¹/₄in) from the edge of the leather, with the stitch line parallel with the zipper teeth (**f**).

8. Open the zipper, place the leather pieces *right sides together* and the lining fabric *right sides together*. Secure with bulldog clips if necessary, then sew around the whole purse 1cm (³/₈in) from the edge. Do NOT sew along the bottom edge of the lining (this will be the opening through which you will turn the purse) (**g**).

9. Trim the corners of the leather to reduce bulk (*see* Techniques: Paring (Skiving)). Turn the leather right sides out though the gap in the lining, and push the corners out as far as possible using a pencil. Then, folding the edges inwards by 1cm (³/₈in), pin and stitch along the gap in the lining fabric (**h**). Remove pins and push lining into the purse.

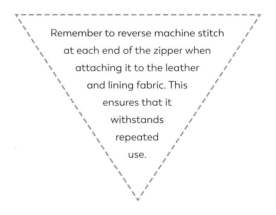

Remember to reverse machine stitch at each end of the zipper when attaching it to the leather and lining fabric. This ensures that it withstands repeated use.

a

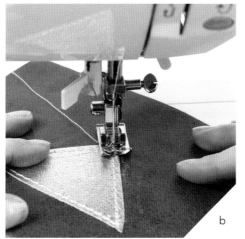

b

c

d

e

f

g

h

To add the leather zipper pull,
thread the piece you cut previously
through the metal zipper end and
punch a hole 1cm (³/₈in) from the
fold. Rivet to secure.

WOMEN'S WALLET

Hold all your cards, notes and coins in one place with this sleek wallet! It may look complicated but is actually straightforward to make following the step-by-step instructions. Try this one when you're confident with your machine sewing.

 Machine sewn

 45 x 22cm (17³/₄ x 8⁵/₈in) piece of vegetable-tanned or stiff chrome-dyed leather, 1.8–2mm thick

You will need:

· Press fastener 15mm (⁵/₈in)
· 15cm (5⁷/₈in) metal zipper

Finished size:

10 x 20cm (4 x 7⁷/₈in) closed
20 x 20cm (7⁷/₈ x 7⁷/₈in) opened

1. Cut out as follows:

- One rectangle 35 x 20cm (13³/₄ x 7⁷/₈in)
- One rectangle 20 x 9cm (7⁷/₈ x 3¹/₂in)

2. Use the scoops and holes template to create a card template to shape and mark the main body (*see* Templates). Align the three scoops on the template with one shorter end of the 35 x 20cm (13³/₄ x 7⁷/₈in) piece of leather and mark the three scoops and hole. Cut out the scoops with a sharp scalpel (*see* Techniques: Cutting) and use a punch to create the hole. Move the template to the opposite short end of the leather and cut away only the *centre scoop* and the hole (**a**).

3. The 20 x 9cm (7⁷/₈ x 3¹/₂in) rectangle is the zipper pocket. Cut out the letterbox window for the zipper around the outside of the marked line on the zipper pocket template (*see* Templates) (**b**).

4. Apply glue around the window on the *wrong side* of the pocket, then around the *right side* of the zipper (make sure you don't get glue too close to the teeth as this will show from the front). Allow glue to go tacky, then carefully stick together making sure the zipper is central in the window (**c**). Machine sew around the window 5mm (¹/₄in) from the edge (**d**).

5. On the edge with three scoops, insert the male part of the press fastener in the hole with the positive part facing upwards on the *right side* of the leather (*see* Techniques: Inserting Fastenings) (**e**).

6. Fold over this end so that the press fastener is just over the fold and therefore on the inside on the wallet (**f**). Holding the fold in place, turn the leather over and use the zipper pocket as a guide to mark a line across the *right side* of the leather just above the fold. Use the edge of the awl or your finger nail to mark this line – avoid using a pen if possible (**g**).

7. Scratch a 5mm (¹/₄in) wide line along the leather above this mark and apply glue along the line (**h**) as well as along the *wrong side* of the bottom edge of the pocket. Stick together once tacky. Stitch along the bottom edge of the pocket to secure it in place (**i**).

a

b

c

d

e

f

g

h

i

8. Starting at the edge of the leather, mark a vertical 4cm (1⅝in) line between each of the three scoops **(j)**. These lines mark where dividers will be sewn later.

9. At the other end, place the female part of the press fastener in place in the remaining hole by the single scoop (*see* Techniques: Inserting Fastenings) **(k)**. Make sure the two parts match up.

10. On the *wrong side* of the leather, apply glue to the short edges of the end pockets, and same length to the back where the pockets will be stuck down. Apply glue where the three scooped pockets will be divided by stitching **(l)**. Once tacky press the two pockets down.

11. Machine sew the vertical 4cm (1⅝in) lines previously marked, making sure the zipper pocket flap is open and therefore not being sewn down. Reverse by two or three stitches at each end or sew two complete rows (double stitch) for consistency **(m)**.

12. To attach the zipper pocket, mark with an awl or your finger nail where the top of the pocket meets the back of the wallet. Scratch a 5mm (¼in) wide line along the leather below this mark and down the two short sides **(n)**.

13. Apply glue to the scratched surface and the edges of the zipper pocket back **(o)**. Wait to go tacky then stick down.

14. Stitch around the three remaining sides of the pocket, with the pocket facing up, and then secure the threads **(p)**.

15. Sew along the two short sides on the front (not the pocket side) of the wallet and secure the threads **(q)**.

16. Wax and burnish the edges if you wish. (*see* Techniques: Surface Finishes).

j

k

l

m

n

o

p

q

Remember to pull threads through to the back of the work, tie them in a knot and burn the ends (*see* Techniques: Machine Sewing) for a secure finish.

MEN'S WALLET

With plenty of space for cards and notes, this wallet is the perfect size for trouser- and jacket-pockets. Meanwhile, the sturdy construction makes it an accessory that will last its owner for years.

 Hand stitched

 28 x 25cm (11 x 9 $^7/_8$in) piece of vegetable-tanned leather, 1.8–2mm thick

You will need:

- Pricking iron 4mm ($^1/_8$in) spacing

Finished size:

9.5 x 12cm (3$^3/_4$ x 4$^3/_4$in)

1. Cut out as follows (**a**):

- One rectangle 24 x 9.5cm (9$\frac{1}{2}$ x 3$\frac{3}{4}$in)
- One rectangle 23.5 x 9.5cm (9$\frac{1}{4}$ x 3$\frac{3}{4}$in)
- Four rectangles each 10 x 5cm (4 x 2in)

2. Create a template to mark the scoops in each of the four pockets (*see* Templates). Use a sharp scalpel to cut the scoops (*see* Techniques: Cutting).

3. On the *wrong side* of the four pockets, pare down (*see* Techniques: Paring (Skiving)) the short sides and bottom edges to thin the leather to roughly half its original thickness (**b**).

4. Place the two back pockets on the right side of the inside piece of the wallet (the inside piece is the slightly narrower of the two large rectangles). Align the outside edge of each pocket with the corresponding outside edge of the wallet, 3cm (1$\frac{1}{8}$in) down from the top edge. Mark around each pocket with the awl, then use sandpaper to scratch away the leather where the pocket will be glued (**c**).

5. On the *wrong side*, apply a thin layer of glue around each of the three edges on each pocket. Also apply it to the *right side* of the inside piece where you have scratched away the leather (**d**). Allow the glue to go tacky, then carefully press the pockets into place.

6. Stitch across the bottom of the two pockets. This can be done by machine to speed up the process, as it will not be visible (**e**).

7. The front pockets will align with the bottom corners of the inside piece. Scratch away the leather for these as before (**e**) apply glue and press in place (**f**).

8. Mark a line 5mm ($\frac{1}{4}$in) in from the inside edge of each pair of pockets using a ruler and awl (**g**).

9. Punch the holes using the 4mm ($\frac{1}{8}$in) pricking iron. Push the awl through each hole to open them up for easier hand stitching (**h**).

10. Clamp the inside piece with the four pockets into the lacing pony with the front side on the left and saddle stitch through the holes you have just created (*see* Techniques: Hand Stitching).

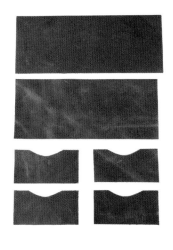

a

b

c

d

e

f

g

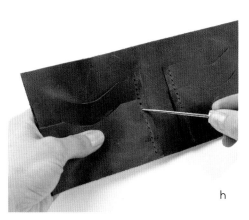

h

When punching holes along
the inside edge of the pockets,
make sure the final hole at the
bottom is no less than 5mm (¼in)
from the edge. The final stitch
should meet the stitching along
the bottom of the wallet, also
5mm (¼in) in from the edge.

11. Lay the inside piece of leather on top of the outside piece *wrong sides together* and mark the gap between pockets with a leather marker pen (i). Apply a strip of glue to the *wrong side* of each piece around the edges to be joined (j). Do not apply glue to the top edge or to the gap you have just marked. You should create a set of mirrored 'L' shapes!

12. Press the inside and outside pieces together carefully, folding the outside piece around the inside piece as you go (k). Once the inner and outer are pressed down all the way around, ensure the edges and corners are firmly secured (l).

13. There may be some excess leather left at one or both of the shorter ends (m). You shouldn't be able to see the wrong side of the leather overhanging from the front or back. To correct this, trim away any excess leather very carefully, using a ruler and sharp scalpel (n). This will ensure a neat finish and make the wallet harder wearing.

14. Mark the hole guideline in that 'L' shape on the outside of the wallet, front and back, and punch the holes as before with the pricking iron. You'll be punching through up to four layers, so angle slightly inwards so that the holes on the back are not too close to the edge of the wallet (o).

15. Go through the holes again with the awl. You will be stitching through several layers of leather so need the holes to be well prepared for hand stitching (*see* Techniques: Hand Stitching) (p).

16. Saddle stitch around the two 'L' shapes (q). When tying off the thread ends, feed each one back through one layer of leather. After they are knotted, cut and burned, the thread ends can be disguised, tucked between the layers.

17. Finish off by burnishing the edges if you wish (*see* Techniques: Surface Treatments).

i

j

k

l

m

n

o

p

q

HANDY PURSES

These little purses are versatile in every way. I've suggested a total quantity of the amount of leather you'll need, but follow my lead – mix and match colours! Choose from two styles – super simple, or with an added gusset to create more capacity.

 Hand stitched

 Option 1:
26 x 22cm (10¹/₄ x 8⁵/₈in) piece of vegetable-tanned or smooth chrome-dyed leather, 1.8–2mm thick

Option 2:
26 x 30cm (10¹/₄ x 11³/₄in) piece of vegetable-tanned or smooth chrome-dyed leather, 1.8–2mm thick

You will need:

· Pricking iron 4mm (¹/₈in) spacing

· Sam Browne stud 5mm (¹/₄in) or press fastener 10–15mm (³/₈–⁵/₈in)

Finished size:

8 x 11cm (3¹/₈ x 4³/₈in)

OPTION 1

SLEEK AND SIMPLE

1. Draw around main body and middle section templates (*see* Templates) onto the *wrong side* of the leather and cut out using a ruler and rotary cutter or scalpel. Use your scalpel to cut out the scoops (**a**). *See* Techniques: Cutting.

2. Mark the folds and holes on the template onto the leather using a leather marker pen. With the pointed flap of the body facing away from you and with the *wrong sides* facing up, apply a thin layer of glue along the three edges of the middle section, and along the corresponding sections of the back of the pocket (**b**). Allow to go tacky then press together.

3. Sand the front two side edges of the *right side* of the middle section to create a key for the glue. Apply glue to the surface of the pocket and to the corresponding areas of the *wrong side* of the purse front (**c**). Allow glue to go tacky, then press together.

4. Using an awl and ruler, score a line 4mm (⅛in) in from the edge on each side of the purse (**d**). Follow these lines to punch the holes using a 4mm (⅛in) pricking iron (**e**). Hold the iron steady as you'll be punching through two different thicknesses of leather where the middle and front sections overlap (*see* Techniques: Scoring & Punching).

5. Place your work in the lacing pony (*see* Techniques: Hand Stitching) and saddle stitch along both sides (**f**).

6. Use a rotary hole puncher to make the hole in the flap for your fastening (*see* Techniques: Inserting Fastenings).

7. Fold the purse closed, then lift the flap slightly to allow for any contents. Mark the position of the second hole on the base of the purse (**g**).

8. Attach the female part of the press fastener to the flap (**h**). Then attach the male part to the front of the purse.

9. Finish by stamping a monogram of your initials if you so wish (*see* Techniques: Embossing).

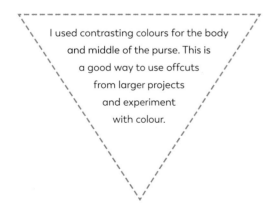

I used contrasting colours for the body and middle of the purse. This is a good way to use offcuts from larger projects and experiment with colour.

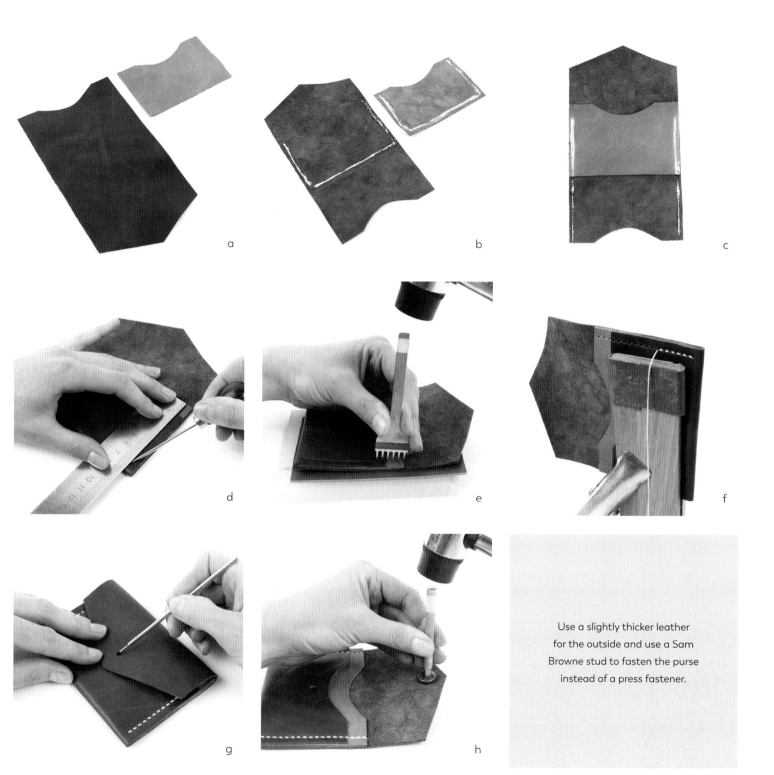

a

b

c

d

e

f

g

h

Use a slightly thicker leather
for the outside and use a Sam
Browne stud to fasten the purse
instead of a press fastener.

OPTION 2

EXTRA SPACE

1. Draw around your templates (*see* Templates) onto the *wrong side* of the leather and cut out using a ruler and rotary cutter or scalpel. I've used different colours for the body, middle section and each gusset piece. Use a scalpel to cut out the scoops (*see* Techniques: Cutting) (**a**). Transfer the folds and holes on the template onto the leather using a leather marker pen.

2. On the main body, apply a thin layer of glue along the three edges of the *wrong side* of the front section. Sand along the edges of the three straight edges on the *right side* of the middle section and apply a thin layer of glue (**b**).

3. Wait a few minutes for the glue to go tacky, then line up and press the front section and middle section together.

4. Loosely position the gusset pieces on the back of the pocket with top corners matching. There should be a gap at the bottom (**c**). Apply glue along each outer edge of the gusset and pocket, allow to go tacky, then press into position.

5. Using an awl and ruler, score a line 4mm (⅛in) in from the edge of the gusset pieces to mark where to punch the holes. The holes will run down the outside edge of each gusset ready for stitching. Punch the holes using the 4mm (⅛in) pricking iron (**d**).

6. Place your work in a lacing pony and saddle stitch through the three layers of leather on each side – gusset piece, middle section and the front of the purse (**e**). *See* Techniques: Hand Stitching.

7. The next stage is a bit fiddly as the purse starts to take shape. Apply glue to the other long edge of each gusset piece and to the corresponding sides of the purse body (**f**), then press them together. Use bulldog clips to hold everything in place until the glue dries (**g**).

8. Punch the holes as before. The other side of the gusset will be in the way a little, so take care to keep the pricking iron correctly positioned (**h**). Put the purse back into the lacing pony and saddle stitch as before (**i**).

9. Use a rotary hole puncher to make the holes for your fastening. Carefully place the tool over the hole marked earlier – check that it lines up correctly before punching the hole.

10. Attach your fastening – either a press fastener or Sam Browne stud (*see* Techniques: Inserting Fastenings).

11. Finish by stamping a monogram of your initials if you so wish.

a

b

c

d

e

f

g

h

i

TABLET CASE

This is simply a much larger version of the Card Holder but because of its size, machine sewing is a much faster way to finish it. With just two long straight lines of stitching, it makes the ideal first machine sewing project. Alternatively it can be hand stitched.

 Machine sewn

 27 x 56cm (10⅝ x 22in) piece of vegetable-tanned or smooth chrome-dyed leather, 1.2–2mm thick

Finished size:
23 x 26cm (9 x 10¼in)

1. Cut out (a):

• One rectangle of leather 23 x 52cm (9 x 20½in)

2. Apply glue along each long edge on the *wrong side* of the leather. A thin layer about 5mm (¼in) wide is plenty. Wait 5–10 minutes for the glue to go tacky (b).

3. Carefully fold the leather in half *wrong sides together*. Make sure the edges are aligned and press together (c). Press along the centre to create a flat even fold (d). Trim off any uneven edges with a sharp scalpel.

4. Set up your sewing machine (*see* Techniques: Machine Sewing). Sew down each side 5mm (¼in) in from the edge, remembering to reverse at each end (e).

5. Mark out the scoop with a leather marker pen and cut with a sharp scalpel (f). You will be cutting through two layers of leather, so cut firmly and carefully. However, cutting both sides at once will give you perfectly matched shapes.

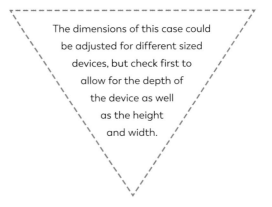

The dimensions of this case could be adjusted for different sized devices, but check first to allow for the depth of the device as well as the height and width.

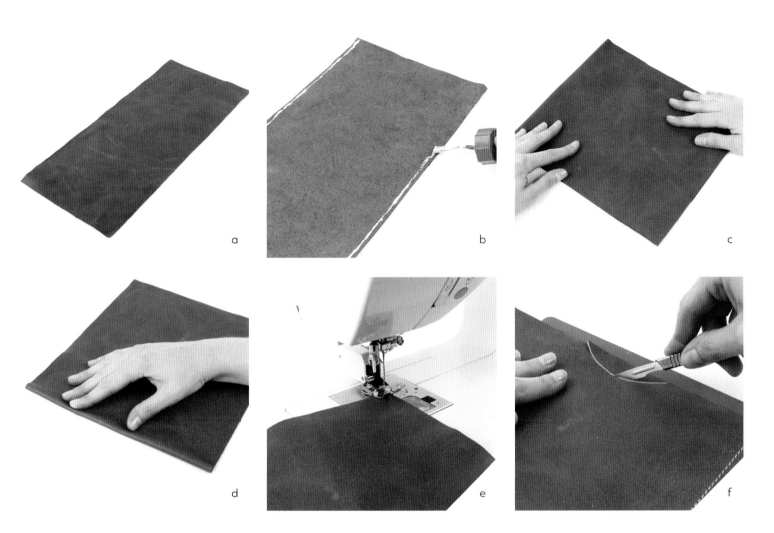

a

b

c

d

e

f

LAPTOP CASE

This is a great item to make when you have perfected your hand stitching. Although a simple shape, getting the size right is essential, especially if you need to adapt the template to fit your laptop. If you are feeling confident, the edge painting creates a stylish finish.

 Hand stitched

 One piece of vegetable-tanned leather, 1.4–2mm thick
See Step 1 to ensure you buy and cut enough leather to fit your size of laptop

You will need:

• Pricking iron 6mm (¼in) spacing

• Two Sam Browne studs 5mm (¼in)

Finished size:

36 x 25cm (14¹/₈ x 9⁷/₈in)

1. The Laptop Case template (*see* Templates) and measurements provided will create a case to fit a laptop measuring 32.5 x 22.7cm (12³/₄ x 9in). You may need to adjust the dimensions of the template to suit the size of your laptop. After measuring your laptop, cut out a template from card and test it around the laptop to ensure that it fits with a 1cm (³/₈in) seam allowance on each side.

2. Use your laptop to check where to fold the leather, allowing for an overlap of 5mm (¹/₄in) (**a**). Mark the join with a leather marker pen and apply glue from the join all the way down the *wrong side* of the leather along each long edge (**b**). (NB stronger impact adhesive might be better than contact adhesive for this project.) Allow the glue to go tacky, then press together. Clamp bulldog clips on each side while the glue dries (**c**).

3. Using an awl and ruler, score a line 5mm (¹/₄in) in from the edge along each side to be stitched (*see* Techniques: Scoring & Punching).

4. Starting approximately 1cm (³/₈in) from the folded lower edge, punch the first set of holes along one side using the pricking iron. Push the awl through all of the holes by 2cm (³/₄in) to make them bigger, as this will ease the hand stitching process (**d**).

5. Select your thread and, with the project secured in a lacing pony, saddle stitch from the overlap all the way along one side (*see* Techniques: Hand Stitching). Repeat this process on the other side (**e**).

6. To position the Sam Browne studs, use the template again, this time to help you mark the flap 2cm (⁷/₈in) in from each edge. Punch the 4mm (¹/₈in) holes as shown (**f**).

7. Put the laptop inside the case and fold over the flap. Use the holes you punched as a guide to mark the corresponding holes on the front of the case (**g**).

8. Punch 3mm (¹/₈in) holes where you have marked (**h**) and screw in the Sam Browne studs (**i**). *See* Techniques: Inserting Fastenings.

9. The edges of the leather can be burnished, painted or a combination of the two. On my example, the stitched sides have been burnished and the flap edges painted with edging paint to match the thread colour. *See* Techniques: Surface Treatments for more information.

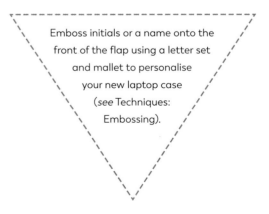

Emboss initials or a name onto the front of the flap using a letter set and mallet to personalise your new laptop case (*see* Techniques: Embossing).

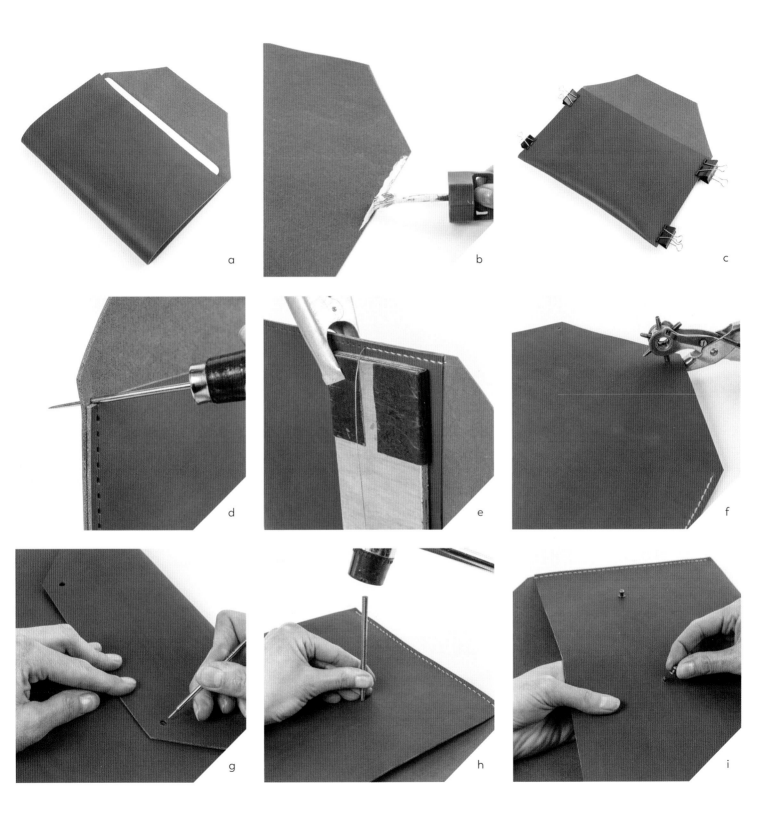

a

b

c

d

e

f

g

h

i

FOLDOVER BAG

The smart design of this bag means you can carry a little or a lot with equal ease. It's suitable for the more confident maker, but as you can also use the bag with or without the strap, you won't mind building the experience needed to tackle this truly versatile design.

 Machine sewn

 52 x 32cm (20¹/₂ x 12⁵/₈in) piece of chrome-dyed leather, 1–1.8mm thick for the top of the bag (main colour)

36 x 32cm (14¹/₈ x 12⁵/₈in) piece of chrome-dyed leather, 1–1.8mm thick for the base of the bag (contrast colour)

120 x 2cm (47¹/₄ x ³/₄in) piece of black vegetable-tanned leather, 2–3mm thick for the strap

You will need:

· Cotton fabric for the lining 80 x 35cm (31¹/₂ x 13³/₄in)

· Metal zipper 23cm (9in)

· Three D-rings 10mm (³/₈in)

· Two lobster clasps 15mm (⁵/₈in)

· Two rivets 6mm (¹/₄in)

Finished size:

34 x 28cm (13³/₈ x 11in) unfolded
20 x 28cm (7⁷/₈ x 11in) folded

1. Cut out as follows (**a**):

• Two rectangles of leather each 30 x 25cm (11³/₄ x 9⁷/₈in) for the top of the bag (main colour – grey)

• Two rectangles of leather each 30 x 14cm (11³/₄ x 5¹/₂in) for the base of the bag (contrast colour – green)

• One square of leather 8cm (3¹/₈in) for the tassel (contrast colour)

• Two squares of leather each 5cm (2in) for the zipper ends (contrast colour)

• Three rectangles of leather each 1 x 6cm (³/₈ x 2³/₈in) for the D-rings and tassel (contrast colour)

• Two rectangles of lining fabric each 30 x 37cm (11³/₄ x 14⁵/₈in)

2. Trim a 1 x 1cm (³/₈ x ³/₈in) triangle from the two corners of each base piece as shown, then apply a 3cm (1¹/₈in) wide strip of glue to the *wrong side* along the top edge (**b**).

3. Once the glue has gone tacky, fold and press down the top edge (**c**).

4. Set up the sewing machine with thread to match or contrast with the leather as preferred. Place the base piece (green) on top of the top piece (grey), overlapping by 1cm (³/₈in) and use masking tape to secure in place. Sew together the two rectangles all the way along the length of the edge (*see* Techniques: Machine Sewing) (**d**). Repeat these steps to create the other side of the bag. Cut a 1 x 1cm (³/₈ x ³/₈in) triangle from each of the remaining two corners of each top piece (**e**).

5. Apply a 3cm (1¹/₈in) wide strip of glue to the *wrong side* along the top edge (**f**). Once the glue has gone tacky, fold and press down as before.

6. To prepare the zipper, take the two small squares of leather, fold in half and glue over each end of the zipper. Covering the fabric part of the zipper only, sew the zipper ends in place (*see* Techniques: Inserting a Zipper).

7. Sew the zipper in place (**g**) – at this stage you will be sewing in the lining fabric too. *See* Techniques: Inserting a Zipper for full instructions on how to do this (**h**).

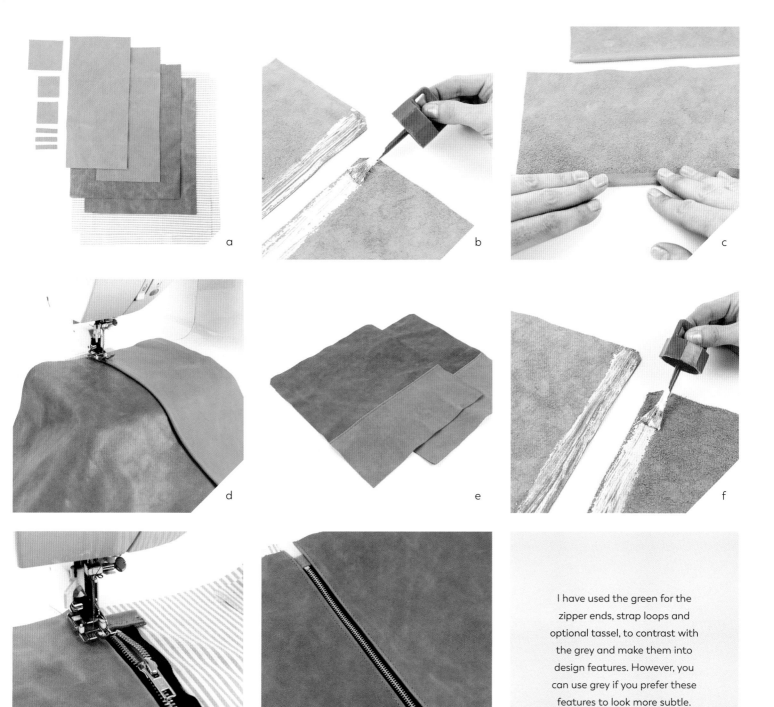

a

b

c

d

e

f

g

h

I have used the green for the zipper ends, strap loops and optional tassel, to contrast with the grey and make them into design features. However, you can use grey if you prefer these features to look more subtle.

8. Take two of the 1 x 6cm (³/₈ x 2³/₈in) strips of leather. Thread each onto a D-ring and apply glue to each side, on the *wrong side* of the leather. Allow to go tacky and press together. These will be the loops onto which you will attach the strap.

9. Sand the *right side* of this leather 1.5cm (⁵/₈in) from the cut edge to create a key for the glue (**i**). Glue the loops in position one-third of the way down the bag, with the cut edges facing *outwards* and flush with the edge of the bag (**j**). You may need to trim the length by about 1cm (³/₈in) so they are not too long.

10. Open the zipper and lay the leather sides *right sides together*, making sure both sides of the lining have been pulled free and that these are also lying *right sides together*. Ensure the loops are still firmly glued in place then secure the edges of the leather with bulldog clips (**k**).

11. Sew all the way around the leather 1cm (³/₈in) in from the edge, and down the two long sides of the lining fabric. Do *not* sew along the bottom edge of the lining – this should be left open for now (**l**).

12. Use a sharp scalpel to trim the seam allowance around the bottom corners of the leather (**m**). This will help to minimise bulk for sharper corners.

13. Measure the distance from the top to the bottom seam on the leather (**n**). Mark the same distance on the lining fabric along the lower edge – this will be the bottom seam line (however do *not* sew up the lining yet).

14. Turn the bag the right way out through the open bottom of the lining (**o**). This is called 'bagging out' and is the exciting part as you see your bag take shape!

15. Push into the inside corners of the leather with the end of a pencil to make the corners as sharp as possible.

16. Fold the open edge of the lining fabric in on itself along the line you previously marked, and topstitch closed (**p**). Push the lining into the bag and smooth out.

17. Add a tassel to the zipper pull. This is simply a smaller version of the Tassel Keyring made using the remaining square and rectangle of leather. Using a D-ring and pliers, attach the finished tassel to the zipper pull.

18. To prepare and attach the strap, follow Steps 17–18 of the Cross-Body Bag (**q**). Your bag is now complete.

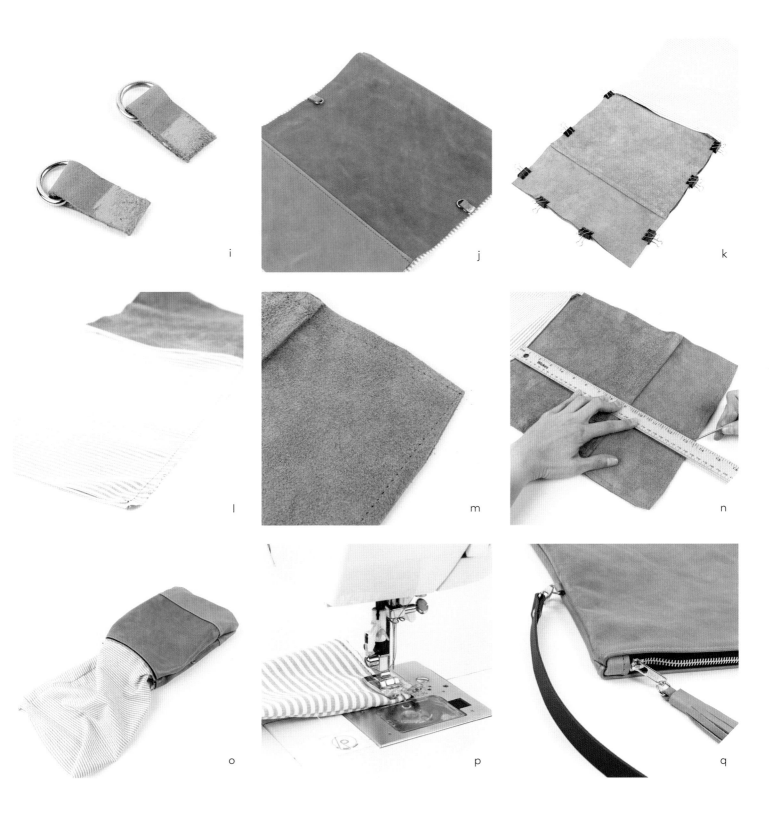

i

j

k

l

m

n

o

p

q

WASH BAG

Wash bags are notoriously tricky to keep clean, but not this one; its waxy material and waterproof lining make it wipe-clean. The design is neutral in shape and colour, so ideal for anyone, while the boxy base will accommodate all your toiletries with ease.

 Machine sewn

 28 x 34cm (11 x 13³/₄in) piece of chrome-dyed leather, 1–1.8mm thick for the base of the bag

You will need:

· Waxed cotton for the top of the bag 30 x 34cm (11³/₄ x 13³/₄in)

· Waterproof fabric for the lining 30 x 65cm (11³/₄ x 25⁵/₈in)

· 23cm (9in) metal zipper

· Rivet 6mm (¹/₄in) for zipper pull (optional)

Finished size:
24 x 18 x 6cm (9¹/₂ x 7¹/₈ x 2³/₈in)

1. Cut out as follows (**a**):

· Two rectangles of leather each 12 x 30cm (4³/₄ x 11³/₄in) for the base of the bag

· Two rectangles of waxed cotton each 14 x 30cm (5¹/₂ x 11³/₄in) for the top of the bag

· Two rectangles of waterproof fabric each 24 x 30cm (9¹/₂ x 11³/₄in) for the lining

2. Trim a 1 x 1cm (³/₈ x ³/₈in) triangle from each of the top two corners of each base piece as shown, then apply a 2cm (³/₄in) wide strip of glue to the *wrong side* along the top edge (**b**). Once the glue has gone tacky, fold and press down the top edge.

3. Place this edge, *right side up*, 1cm (³/₈in) over the corresponding edge of the *right side* of the waxed cotton (**c**). You cannot tape them together due to the waxy finish so use bulldog clips at each end.

4. Set up the sewing machine with thread to match or contrast with the leather as preferred, and stitch together the two rectangles all the way along the length of the edge (*see* Techniques: Machine Sewing). Keep stopping to check the leather and waxed cotton are still in line and always reverse at the beginning and end of your stitching (**d**).

5. Repeat these steps to create the other side of the bag.

6. Attach a zipper foot to your sewing machine. Apply glue to the ends of the zipper on the back and fold each side outwards (**e**).

7. Align the zipper with the top edge of the lining fabric (on the fabric's waterproof *right side*) with the zipper pull on the right. Sew the edge of the zipper along the edge of the lining fabric 5mm (¹/₄in) from the edge. *See* Techniques: Inserting a Zipper for more tips.

8. Trim a 1 x 1cm (³/₈ x ³/₈in) triangle from each of the top two corners of each waxed cotton piece, then apply a 2cm (³/₄in) wide strip of glue to the *wrong side* along the top edge. Once the glue has gone tacky, fold and press down the top edge.

9. Place the folded edge of the waxed cotton *right side up* on top of the stitched zipper and pin in place (**f**). Sew along 5mm (¹/₄in) from the edge of the leather ensuring that the stitch line remains parallel with the zipper teeth. Repeat this process to complete the other side of the bag and attach it to the other side of the zipper.

10. Open the zipper and place the two sides of the bag *right sides together*. Use clips to keep the sides lined up around the leather as shown (**g**).

11. Sew all the way around the bag 1cm (³/₈in) in from the edge (**h**), and down the two sides of the lining. Sew only 5cm (2in) in from each corner of the bottom edge of the lining fabric, leaving a gap approximately 18cm (7¹/₈in) wide in the middle for bagging out.

a

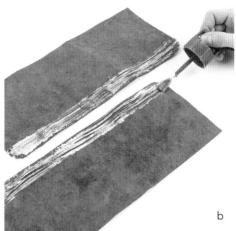

b

c

d

e

f

g

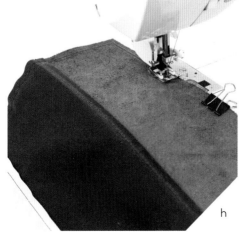

h

Although you need to leave a gap in the lining for turning, it's important to sew some of the way along from the corners as instructed to allow you to form the boxy base at the next stage.

12. Pinch the corners of the lining open and lie flat, matching the seam edges. Mark a line 2.5cm (1in) in from the seam line (*not* the edge). You should now be able to mark a line 5cm (2in) across from edge to edge (**i**).

13. Sew across this line then cut away the excess corner to reduce bulk (**j**). Repeat with the other lining corner, then with the two leather corners (**k**).

14. Pull the bag out through the opening in the lining, and pull everything right sides out (**l**). This is called 'bagging out'.

15. Fold the open edge of the lining in on itself and topstitch closed (**m**). Push the lining into the bag and smooth out.

16. If you would like to add a zipper pull tab, cut a rectangle from scrap leather approximately 10cm (4in) long by the width of the gap in the zipper pull. Cut the ends at an angle, thread through the zipper pull and rivet in place (*see* Techniques: Inserting Fastenings) (**n**).

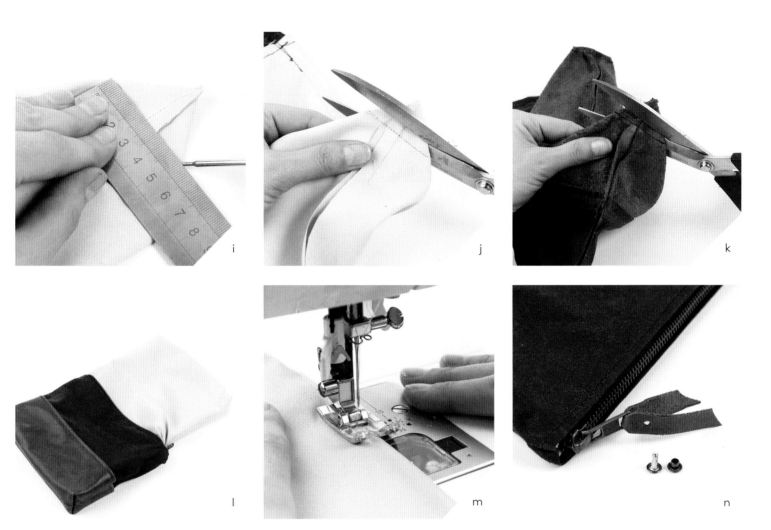

i

j

k

l

m

n

CROSS-BODY BAG

This is a versatile bag for the more advanced maker. The modern design incorporates metallic elements for an elegant look, while the removable strap allows it to be used as a chic clutch for the evening or with the shoulder strap for hands-free daytime use.

 Machine sewn

 80 x 45cm (31$\frac{1}{2}$ x 17$\frac{3}{4}$in) piece of chrome-dyed leather, 1–1.8mm thick for the body of the bag

28 x 15cm (11 x 5$\frac{7}{8}$in) piece of metallic gold chrome-dyed leather, 1–1.8mm thick for large triangle

23 x 11cm (9 x 4$\frac{3}{8}$in) piece of black chrome-dyed leather, 1–1.8mm thick for small triangle

120 x 2cm (47$\frac{1}{4}$ x $\frac{3}{4}$in) piece of black vegetable-tanned leather, 2–3mm thick for the strap

You will need:

· 80 x 45cm (31$\frac{1}{2}$ x 17$\frac{3}{4}$in) piece of cotton fabric for the lining

· Metal zipper 23cm (9in)

· Two D-rings 10mm ($\frac{3}{8}$in)

· Four rivets 6mm ($\frac{1}{4}$in)

· Two lobster clasps 15mm ($\frac{5}{8}$in)

Finished size:

35 x 19cm (13$\frac{3}{4}$ x 7$\frac{1}{2}$in)

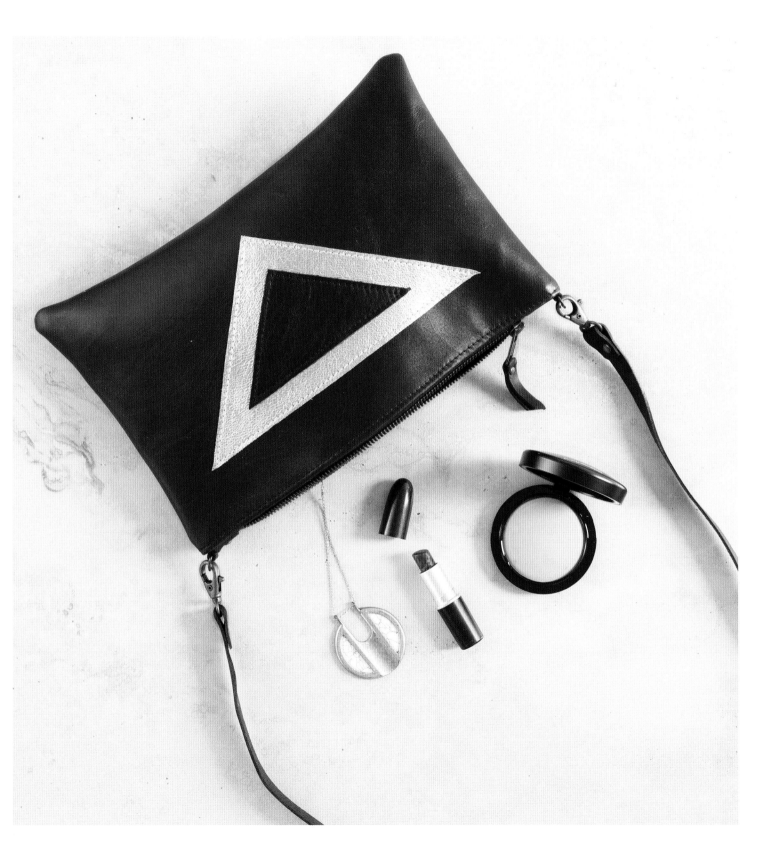

1. Cut out as follows (**a**):

• Two rectangles of chrome-dyed leather each 37.5 x 21cm (14³/₄ x 8¹/₄in) for the body of the bag

• Two squares of chrome-dyed leather each 5cm (2in) for the zipper ends

• Two strips of chrome-dyed leather each 1 x 6cm (³/₈ x 2³/₈in) for strap loops

• One strip of chrome-dyed leather 10 x 1cm (4 x ³/₈in) for the zipper pull (optional)

• Two rectangles of lining fabric each 37.5 x 21cm (14³/₄ x 8¹/₄in)

• One large metallic gold chrome-dyed leather triangle for the embellishment (*see* Templates)

• One small black chrome-dyed leather triangle for the embellishment (*see* Templates)

2. Apply glue to the *wrong side* of the large metallic gold chrome-dyed leather triangle and to the corresponding area in the centre of the *right side* of one of the leather rectangles. Ensure that the triangle point is in the middle and that the triangle is positioned slightly higher to allow for the seam allowance at the bottom. When the glue is tacky, press the glued sides together (**b**).

3. Set up your sewing machine (*see* Techniques: Machine Sewing) with cream or gold thread and sew in place (**c**).

4. Repeat the process to glue and sew the small black triangle centrally on top of the gold triangle, using black thread (**d**).

5. Turn the two leather rectangles *wrong side* up and pare each one down around the edges to remove bulk (**e**). *See* Techniques: Paring (Skiving).

6. Apply a 3cm (1¹/₈in) wide strip of glue to the *wrong side* along the top edge of both the front and back panel of the bag. Allow to go tacky, then fold the edge over by 1cm (³/₈in) (**f**).

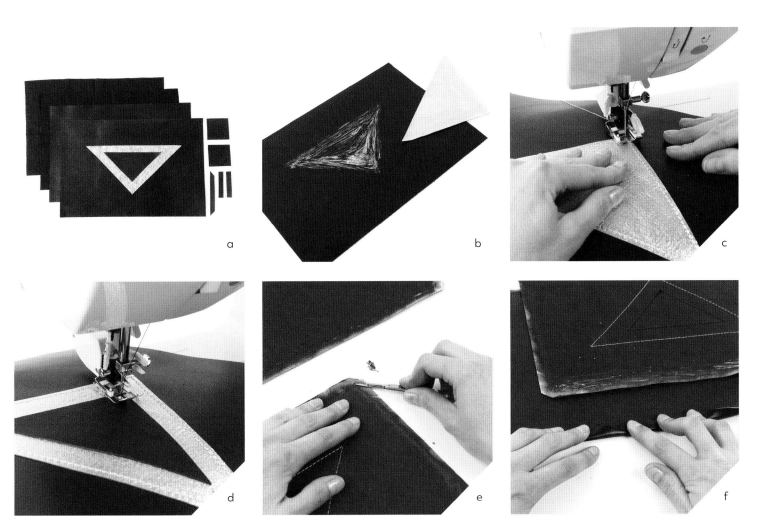

a

b

c

d

e

f

7. To prepare the zipper, take the two 5cm (2in) squares of leather, fold in half and glue over each end of the zipper, covering the fabric part only (the leather shouldn't touch the metal part of the zipper). Sew across the edge of the leather to secure in place (g).

8. Sew the zipper in place – at this stage you will be sewing in the lining fabric too (*see* Techniques: Inserting a Zipper) (h).

9. Open the zipper and lay the leather sides *right sides together*, making sure both sides of the lining have been pulled free and are also lying *right sides together* Secure the edges of the leather with bulldog clips (i).

10. Sew all the way around the three edges of the leather 1cm ($^3/_8$in) in from the edge.

11. Measure the distance from the top to the bottom seam on the leather (j) and mark the same distance on the lining fabric to show the stitch line. Sew down the two short sides of the lining, leaving the bottom edge open for now.

12. Turn the bag the right way out through the open bottom of the lining. This is called 'bagging out' and is the most exciting part as you see your bag take shape (k)!

13. Push into the inside corners of the leather with the end of a pencil to make the corners as crisp as possible.

14. Fold the open edge of the lining in on itself along the line you previously marked and topstitch closed. Push the lining into the bag and smooth out.

15. Take the two 1 x 6cm ($^3/_8$ x $2^3/_8$in) strips of leather. Thread each onto a D-ring and apply glue to each end, on the *wrong side* of the leather (l). Allow glue to go tacky, then press together. These will be the loops onto which the strap will be attached.

16. Punch a hole in the tab at each end of the zipper and also in each loop tab (m). Push the loop tab into the gap at the end of the bag and rivet the tab and zipper end together. Repeat on the other side. *See* Techniques: Inserting Fastenings.

17. For the strap, take the piece of black vegetable-tanned leather and set the strap cutter 15mm ($^5/_8$in) wide (or as wide as the lobster clasps you have). Cut one 110cm ($43^1/_4$in) length of leather with a strap cutter (*see* Techniques: Cutting).

18. Round off each end with a belt-end cutter (*see* Techniques: Rounding Off Ends). Pull the strap through the lobster clasp by 3cm ($1^1/_8$in), fold over, punch a hole and rivet in place on each end (n). Clip the strap onto the bag.

19. If you want to, add the zipper pull as the finishing touch (o).

You can adjust the length of the strap depending on your own preference. If your leather is not long enough, glue and rivet two shorter pieces together.

g

h

i

j

k

l

m

n

o

ENVELOPE CLUTCH

I love to work with simple designs that have a dramatic effect. This clutch requires just a few steps but the outcome looks as if it took much longer than it did! This is a good project to do on the sewing machine if you are a beginner or fairly new to sewing with leather.

Machine sewn

50 x 35cm (19³/₄ x 13³/₄in) piece of vegetable-tanned leather or stiff chrome-dyed leather, 1.8–2mm thick for the main body of the bag

35 x 18cm (13³/₄ x 7¹/₈in) piece of vegetable-tanned leather or stiff chrome-dyed leather, 1.8–2mm thick for the side panels of the bag (either the same leather as the main body, or in a contrast colour)

You will need:

· Sam Browne stud 5–6mm (¹/₄in)

Finished size:

30 x 20cm (11³/₄ x 7⁷/₈in)

1. Use the templates (see Templates) to cut one main body piece and two triangle side panels (a).

2. On the wrong side of the main body, measure 4cm (1⅝in) down from the base of the triangle. Mark a line with an awl across as shown (b). Repeat at the other end of the main body. This is where the leather will fold on the top and bottom of the bag.

3. Position the side panels in place with their longer 20cm (7⅞in) sides aligned with the angled sides at one end of the main body. When aligned with the fold mark made in the previous step, the centre points should touch in the middle and the point of the lower flap shows as a small diamond shape (c).

4. On the right side of the side panels, mark and scratch the surface where the leather will be joined and apply glue to each surface in a strip 1.5–2cm (⅝–¾in) wide. Apply glue to the wrong side of the main body along the corresponding edges (d). Allow the glue to go tacky, then press the pieces together.

5. Machine sew the side panels in place 5mm (¼in) from the edge to form an inverted 'V' shape (e). Stop sewing 5mm (¼in) from each end.

6. Fold along the score line wrong sides together and mark the join where the tip of the side panels meet the main body on the edges. Apply a strip of glue 1cm (⅜in) along these edges, between the two points (f). Leave to go tacky then press together, securing with bulldog clips while it dries.

7. Machine sew along each side 5mm (⅝in) from the edge (g), finishing just before the lower edge of the bag. The stitching on the sides will meet with the stitching on the inverted 'V' as shown (h). Pull the threads through to the back, cut and burn (see Techniques: Machine Sewing).

8. Fold the top flap over to check the overlap and mark out where to punch a hole for the Sam Browne stud. Punch the hole in the bottom half of the purse (i) and screw in the stud (see Techniques: Inserting Fastenings) .

9. Line up the top flap with the Sam Browne stud. Remember to allow a bit of space for the purse to close when it is full – about 5–10mm (¼–⅜in) – and mark the position for the corresponding hole. Punch a hole 4.5mm (⅛in) in size. If the stud doesn't fit through the hole, carefully add a slit using a scalpel on the top side of the hole to make it bigger (see Techniques: Inserting Fastenings).

a

b

c

d

e

f

g

h

i

UPCYCLED TOTE

I love making bags from items that are no longer worn, such as jackets. Giving a gorgeous material a new lease of life with a unique pattern means no two bags are ever the same. This project is for a simple tote bag; when upcycling products with existing seams, it's best to keep the shape as simple as possible. Good luck!

 Machine sewn

 A leather jacket, preferably a large one, with minimal details and soft leather

Vegetable-tanned leather, 2–3mm thick for the straps

You will need:

· Cotton fabric for the lining

· Medium- or heavy-weight iron-on interfacing

· Metal zipper 15–20cm (5^7/$_8$–7^7/$_8$in) (optional)

· Eight rivets 9mm (³/₈in) for straps

Finished size:

35 x 39cm (13³/₄ x 15³/₈in)

1. Photograph the jacket before you dismantle it – you want to impress your friends and post 'before and after' Instagram shots when you're done (a)!

2. Carefully cut off the sleeves at the top of the seam (unpicking the seams takes too long) (b). These can be put away to make straps or another bag entirely.

3. Cut away the lining fabric. If worth saving, cut economically to put away for a future project. Otherwise, discard. I used the back panel leather only, so cut away the front left and right panels along the seams (c). I also cut away the collar, and put these pieces away for future use.

4. You should be left with a large, roughly rectangular piece of leather (d). If you need to remove buttons or other details, be careful not to rip the leather.

5. Trim the edges to make an even rectangle (e). This piece ended up being 85 x 50cm (33$\frac{1}{2}$ x 19$\frac{3}{4}$in). It will be folded in half to make the bag, with the folded edge forming the base. Remember that the width will narrow once the gusset is built into the base, and it will lose 1.5cm ($\frac{5}{8}$in) each side for the seam allowance.

6. Cut the interfacing to fit within a seam allowance of 1.5cm ($\frac{5}{8}$in) along the short edges, and to fit exactly up to the edge of the leather along the long sides. So for this bag, I cut it 82 x 50cm (32$\frac{1}{4}$ x 19$\frac{3}{4}$in). Iron the interfacing onto the *wrong side* of the leather, following the manufacturer's instructions. This is likely to be an uneven surface due to the jacket seams so work the iron carefully around the seams for the best possible adhesion (f). Once cool, check that the corners are stuck down – if not, repeat with the iron or use glue.

7. Using the leather as a template (g), cut the lining fabric to exactly the same size. In this case 85cm x 50cm (33$\frac{1}{2}$ x 19$\frac{3}{4}$in).

8. Next cut your fabric for the pocket (h). For this bag, my zipper is 20cm (7$\frac{7}{8}$in) wide so the pocket fabric is 24 x 40cm (9$\frac{1}{2}$ x 15$\frac{3}{4}$in). This size is the result of adding 4cm (1$\frac{1}{2}$in) to the length of the zipper for the width, and my preference for the depth of pocket for the length.

9. I added a leather trim (collar) around the zipper. Use the template (*see* Templates) to cut a collar from a leftover piece from the jacket (i). I used a 20cm (7$\frac{7}{8}$in) zipper, but if yours is a different length simply adapt the template to suit.

I often scour charity shops or eBay for good leather jackets. Avoid spending more than £10 if you can, unless it's just too gorgeous to resist!

10. Lay the lining fabric *wrong side* up, with the short edge along the top. Measure 10cm (4in) in from the top short edge and 25cm (9⁷⁄₈in) in from one long edge. Then measure 9.5cm (3³⁄₄in) either side of this point, marking a 19cm (7¹⁄₂in) line. Mark a 5mm (¹⁄₄in) 'V' shape at the each end of the line (j).

11. Apply a 1cm (³⁄₈in) wide strip of glue around the line and allow it to become tacky. Using a ruler and scalpel, cut along the line, and cut a small 'V' shape at each end.

12. Carefully fold the two horizontal sides back (k) (the 'V' cuts allow this). The window should be 10–12mm (³⁄₈–¹⁄₂in) deep to fit the zipper; any more and the zipper cannot be sewn in securely. Sew the sides down making sure they are even.

13. Apply glue to the back of the leather collar 5mm (¹⁄₄in) in from the edge and around the front of the zipper (l). Ensure no glue will be visible through the window, then stick together.

14. Apply glue to the outside edge of the back of the collar, and on the *right side* of the fabric around the window in a 5mm (¹⁄₄in) wide strip (m). Leave to go tacky and stick in place with the zipper open to make sure it lines up with the window.

15. Stitch all around the outer edge of the collar 5mm (¹⁄₄in) from the edge (n). (*See Techniques: Machine Sewing*).

16. Lay the pocket fabric *right side down* with the short edge along the bottom of the zipper edge on the *wrong side* and tape in place as shown (o). Sew the bottom edge only on the machine (p).

17. Fold the pocket *right sides together* with the top edge covering the top edge of the zipper (q). Tape in place, then stitch around the remaining three sides of the zipper *right side up* (r).

You can leave out the collar or the pocket if you wish. However, in large bags it is always useful to have an internal pocket; it's more effort but well worth it!

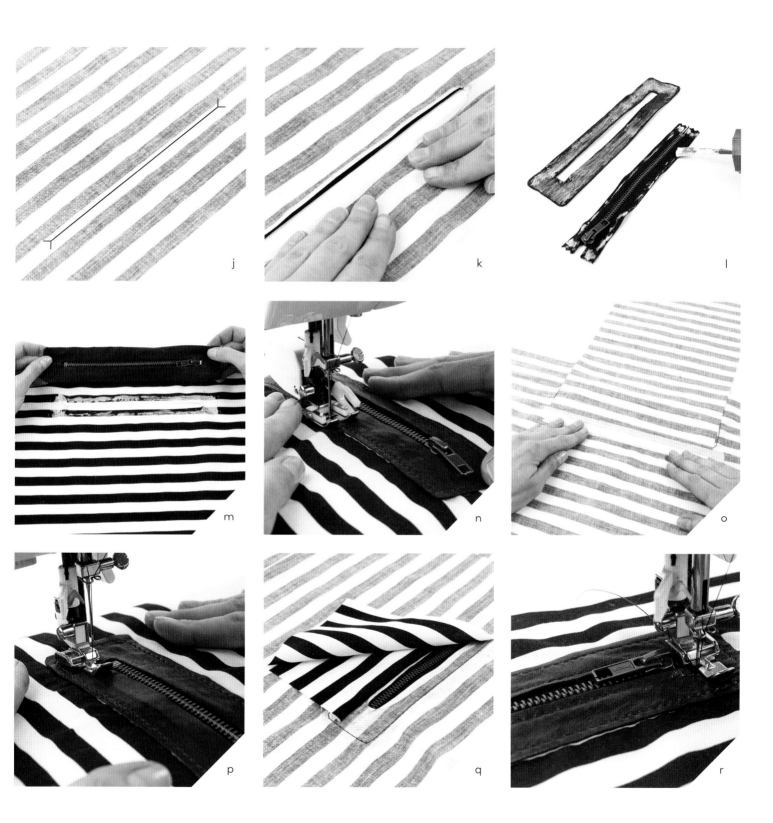

j

k

l

m

n

o

p

q

r

18. Fold the lining away from the pocket before sewing up each side of the pocket leaving it fully enclosed (s). Sew through the pocket only – don't catch the lining!

19. Place fabric and leather *right sides together* (t), clip in place and sew along the edge of the interfacing (where you left a seam allowance) on the top and bottom only (u). Then pull apart in the middle to match up the fabric *right sides together* and leather *right sides together* (v).

20. With the top edges in line with each other on the front and back of the bag, stitch down one side starting at the fold in the leather, 1.5cm (⁵/₈in) in from the edge. Continue along to the fold in the lining fabric (w). Repeat on the other side, but *sew only one-third of the way down* the lining as you need to leave a gap for turning later!

21. I added 'box' corners to give the bag a more 3D shape. *See* the Wash Bag for detailed instructions on how to create these. In this example, I wanted the depth of the flat bottom to be 8cm (3¹/₈in) so I measured 4cm (1⁵/₈in) from seam to edge each way to create a triangle and sewed across perpendicular to the bag seam. Repeat for the other bag outer corner and each lining corner. I trimmed 1cm (³/₈in) from each corner to reduce bulk.

22. Apply a thin layer of glue all the way along the seam allowance on the *wrong side* of the leather at the top of the bag, and the same width on the other side of the seam along the interfacing (x). This strip of glue will help the seam allowance lie flat around the opening of the bag.

23. Pull the bag through the gap in the lining and turn it in on itself. Pin and sew up the gap in the lining, then push the lining into the bag and use a pencil to push it into the corners to create a crisply shaped bottom!

24. Topstitch all the way around the top edge of the bag 3mm (¹/₈in) from the edge (y). This is where you previously applied glue to the wrong side of the seam allowance. The combination of glue and stitching creates a crisp, even finish around the opening.

25. To make the straps, take a strap cutter (*see* Techniques: Cutting) and set to 2cm (³/₄in) wide. Cut two strips of vegetable-tanned leather 70cm (27¹/₂in) long (or to your desired length). Cut 1cm (³/₈in) off the ends with a belt-end cutter (optional).

26. Punch a hole 1cm (³/₈in) and 4cm (1⁵/₈in) from each end of the straps for the rivets. On the front of the bag, place the straps 6cm (2³/₈in) over the edge and line up so they are the same distance from the centre. Mine are 8cm (3¹/₈in) either side of the centre so the space between the straps is 16cm (6¹/₄in), measured from the inside of the straps.

27. Once happy with the position, use the straps to mark the holes (z), then use the punch. Repeat for the back of the bag, then rivet the straps in place making sure they are not twisted (zz). You are finished!

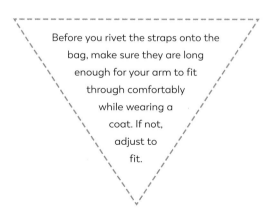

Before you rivet the straps onto the bag, make sure they are long enough for your arm to fit through comfortably while wearing a coat. If not, adjust to fit.

s

t

u

v

w

x

y

z

zz

TECHNIQUES

Successful and creative leatherwork requires a few basic techniques. They may seem daunting at first, but by starting with the simpler projects in this book you'll be able to learn and practise them as you go. By gradually building up your skills, you'll feel your confidence growing too, allowing you to move on to the more complex techniques.

CUTTING

Leather must be cut accurately to achieve the best results. Remember the rule – measure twice, cut once!

CUTTING BASICS

1. Mark around the template with a leather marker pen, pressing down firmly on the template with your free hand so that is does not move (a). Alternatively, use a ruler to measure and mark the lines to be cut (b).

2. Place the ruler – a safety ruler if you have one – along the line and cut with a rotary cutter (ideal for thinner leather that can stretch) or sharp scalpel (c).

CUTTING OUT SCOOPS

Scoops can be cut freehand, but make and use a template as a guide if it helps. It is best to cut in one smooth movement using a sharp scalpel. Press firmly as you cut (but not *too* hard as this can cause the blade to snap!) (d). Scoops can also be cut using a belt-end cutter (e) (*see* Techniques: Rounding Off Ends).

CUTTING STRAPS

A strap cutter is used to cut vegetable-tanned leather straps and belts. It is an accurate and quick way to make strips of leather of even width, and so a crucial part of your tool kit if you make bags or belts on a regular basis. Ensure that the leather stays flat against the side of the cutter and the width remains even all the way along (f).

a

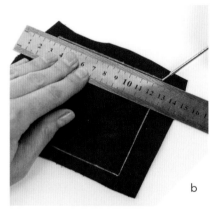

b

If you have one, use a rotary cutter for straight lines and a scalpel for curves and awkward shapes. This will keep your blades sharp.

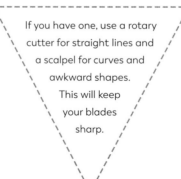

c

ROUNDING OFF ENDS

A rounded end creates a neat finish and professional effect, so it's worth mastering the technique.

USING A BELT-END CUTTER

These cutters come in many shapes and sizes, and give the cleanest finish. I have them in various widths (a) and recommend that you have at least one in your kit. You will need one 2cm (³⁄₄in) or 2.5cm (1in) wide for most projects in this book.

1. Make sure the width of leather you are cutting is slightly narrower than the tool to avoid cutting unwanted notches out of your piece.

2. Mark where you wish the rounded end to be, then place the tool over the mark with a nylon mat underneath to avoid damaging your work surface. Ensure the tool is facing in the correct direction.

3. Hold the tool near the base and hit with a mallet or hammer (b) until it has cut through the leather (c). Don't angle the tool or you will leave a bevelled edge on the leather that you don't want.

d

e

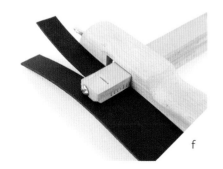

f

a

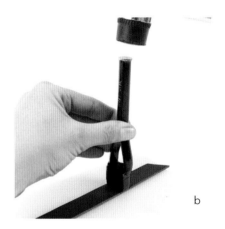

b

c

USING A TEMPLATE AND SCALPEL

A cheaper alternative to a special cutter is to use a template and scalpel.

1. Mark out the leather to be cut off using a template, then cut away the majority with a single slice.

2. Tidy up all the way around the first cut line to create a smooth curve (d).

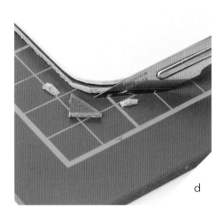

d

Try not to get carried away as you tidy up around the edge; if you are not careful you can easily cut away *too* much!

PARING (SKIVING)

Occasionally you will need to make an area or piece of leather thinner to allow for folding, layering or fitting. It's a clever technique that's invaluable for a neat finish.

USING A SCALPEL

With a sharp scalpel blade, shave off leather on the *wrong side* around the edges as instructed in the project (a). This will thin the leather and remove bulk, especially important where multiple layers will be built up, such as wallet pockets. Paring some leathers, particularly chrome-dyed leather, will reveal lighter colours underneath.

USING A PARING TOOL

If you have a paring tool like the one shown (b), you might find it easier to use than a scalpel. It's particularly effective on areas such as belt ends where the piece you are working on is narrow.

THINNING CORNERS

Pare leather along edges and corners where thicker or stiffer leather is being 'bagged out' (c). Removing bulk leather in these small areas helps create crisper corners, in bags especially.

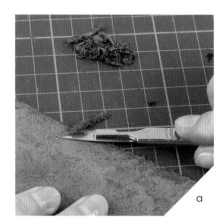

a

b

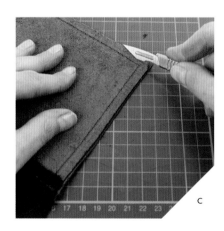

c

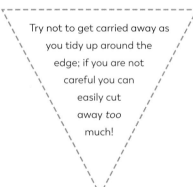

SCORING & PUNCHING

When marking lines on leather for a row of stitch holes, measure your line evenly along the edge of the leather, 4–5mm (1/8–1/4in) from the edge.

USING A RULER AND AWL

Crease rather than *scratch* your line in the leather. Hold the ruler steady, applying pressure from above to stop it slipping. Draw the awl firmly but carefully along the ruler to leave an indent rather than a scratch (**a**).

USING A CREASER

A creaser literally makes a crease or indentation in the leather. This is good for marking curved items, and on thick and vegetable-tanned leather where the crease is easier to make and see (**b**).

Now you're ready to make the holes...

On some very smooth leathers a creaser tool can slip, so I suggest using a ruler and awl for the maximum control.

a

b

USING A PRICKING IRON

Once you have a line, use your pricking iron and mallet to punch a row of holes (**c**). The project will tell you which size to use.

1. Put some thick leather underneath your project to help the prongs go all the way through your work, and to protect your cutting mat from getting covered in holes.

2. Place the iron at the beginning of the line, hold vertically and hit firmly with the mallet until it has gone all the way through the leather.

3. As you work your way along the line, use the last hole punched with the iron as a guide for where to position the iron next.

WIDENING THE HOLES

After you have punched your holes with the pricking iron, push the awl through each hole to gently stretch it (**d**). This helps the needles pass through more easily when hand stitching.

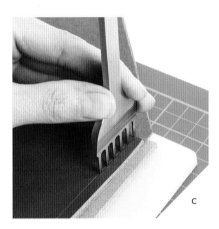

c

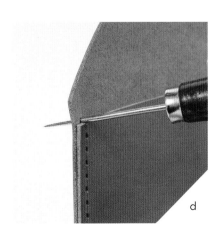

d

GLUING

The process of gluing leather is essential for strength and accuracy in construction. There are just a few simple techniques to remember.

GLUING THE RIGHT SIDE

1. The right side, or top, of leather often has a shiny or non-porous surface. So, when gluing onto this side you will need to create a 'key' onto which the glue can adhere. Use a small piece of sandpaper to carefully scratch off the top layer of leather where glue is to be applied **(a)**.

2. Apply a thin layer of latex glue (such as Copydex) to both pieces being joined. Allow the glue to dry until clear and tacky – this takes around 5–10 minutes **(b)**.

3. Carefully press the pieces together, or fold the edge over **(c)**, as instructed. Take care to be accurate and try to avoid readjusting the bond.

EXTRA STRONG ADHESIVE

When the leather is very thick or stiff, or needs a stronger glue, use a specialist formula such as Evo-Stik impact adhesive. Apply in the same way as Copydex, leaving it to dry for a couple of minutes until it goes tacky. Then press the pieces together and clamp until dry **(d)**.

If you clamp your work while the glue dries, ensure you protect the leather from getting marked by the jaws.

a

c

b

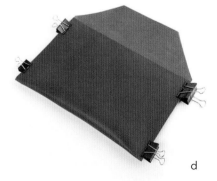

d

HAND STITCHING

Hand stitching leather is simple once you have prepared the holes (*see* Techniques: Scoring & Punching). The projects in this book use the traditional leather craft technique of saddle stitch.

1. Measure the length of the area to be stitched. Multiply this number by four to give you the length of thread needed: e.g. if the length to be stitched is 15cm (5⅞in), you will need 60cm (23⅝in) of thread.

2. If you have a lacing pony, secure your leatherwork with the top side facing left. Thread a needle on each end of the thread, leaving tails 10cm (4in) each end. Pull the needle through the first hole from left to right (a) and even up the lengths.

3. Feed the *left* needle through the next hole along, away from you, from left to right and pull it tight. Then push the *right* needle through the *same* hole underneath the thread, pulling both needles to tighten the stitching (b). Repeat all the way along the row of holes (c).

4. When you reach the end, complete two more stitches in reverse (or over the first two if you have completed a loop) (d).

Then push the left thread through the next hole along so both threads are on the right side (back) of your item.

5. Take your work out of the lacing pony and cut the thread end down to about 3mm (⅛in) long.

6. Burn the ends of the thread with a lighter or matches so they melt down into small lumps (e). Press the lumps flat, being careful not to burn yourself, to finish.

c

a

d

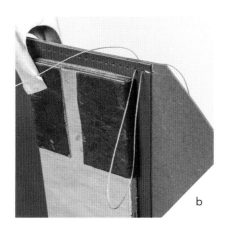

b

e

MACHINE SEWING

Some of the larger projects in this book require machine sewing. If you know the basics of using a sewing machine, then adapting it to sew on leather is easy.

TIPS FOR USING A MACHINE

· You can easily buy the foot and needles needed to adapt your sewing machine for sewing leather (*see* Tool Box: Specialist Leather Craft Tools).

· Always do a test on scrap leather first. Unlike fabric, leather shows needle holes so you can't really disguise mistakes!

· Change your leather needle back to a standard fabric needle when sewing linings and other fabrics. Leather needles will 'cut' fabric and weaken the seams.

· Reverse stitch at the beginning and end of your stitching to secure the thread and strengthen the join. Pull the threads through to the back, trim and burn the ends as for hand stitching leather (*see* Techniques: Hand Stitching).

INSERTING FASTENINGS

Metal studs and press fasteners are an effective and attractive way to secure leather bags and purses. Once you've decided on your favourite type of fastener, it's worth investing in good quality tools to attach them as you'll use these time and time again.

PUNCHING THE HOLE

No matter what type of fastening you use, a hole has to be created in the leather to hold it in place.

1. Mark the position of the fastening using a leather marker pen. The position will be indicated on the template or instructions, and the diameter will depend on the size of fastener used (always check the manufacturer's instructions). If using a rotary hole puncher, set it to the required diameter and punch the hole, squeezing the punch firmly in a single smooth movement (**a**).

2. If the position for the hole is inaccessible with the rotary hole puncher, use a separate hole punching tool with a mallet, placing a nylon mat directly underneath. Hit with the mallet until the tool has cut through the leather (**b**).

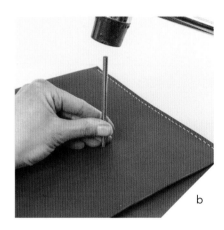

a

b

The leather will stretch a little, so it's best to start with the hole slightly smaller than the width of the fastening.

SAM BROWNE STUDS

These simple studs are easy to insert and provide a minimalist, elegant finish.

1. Push the screw end up through the hole in the body of the project and tighten the stud on top by hand (c).

2. Punch a corresponding hole in the flap or use a scalpel to cut a cross shape. The stud should fit snugly to begin with as the leather will stretch a little (d).

PRESS FASTENERS

With a satisfying 'snap' these fasteners take a little more work but are worth it.

1. You need three tools and four parts for the fastener as shown. To begin, punch the required hole in the leather (e).

2. Take the two male parts of the fastener and place the stud up through the hole in the body of the project. Place the metal disc under the stud to protect the back of your work. Place the 'nipple' part on top on the *right side* of the leather. Take the wider or recessed tool and place over the 'nipple'. Hit with the hammer until secure (f).

3. Repeat with the remaining parts (female) and the other tool on the flap. Hammer in place, taking care not to damage the spring components (g).

4. Test your popper is secure (it should not spin round). Your fastener is complete (h).

f

c

g

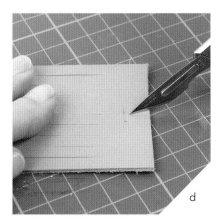

d

e

h

RIVET FASTENINGS

Rivets create a strong, permanent fastening for attaching bag straps, making belts and attaching zipper pulls.

1. Punch the required hole, taking extra care as you will probably be punching through at least two layers of leather (i). You may want to clip the layers in place to stop them slipping as you press down.

2. Ensure the leather is in place around the zipper pull, D-ring or other feature *before* riveting in place (j)!

3. Place the double capped rivet through the hole and set using a press tool such as the table mounted rivet tool shown (*see* Tool Box: Specialist Leather Craft Tools) to secure in place (k). If you do not have one of these you can use a hand tool (*see* Resources) or a hammer kit.

i

j

k

INSERTING A ZIPPER

Adding a zipper to leather bags and purses not only means that they close securely, but the hardware also looks smart, adding another design feature to your project.

1. Put a standard fabric sewing needle and a zipper foot onto your sewing machine before you begin.

2. Pin your zipper *right side up* along the top edge of your lining fabric (also *right side up*) and the zipper pull on the right hand side. Sew along the edge of the zipper – not touching the teeth – with matching coloured thread (a).

3. Change the needle to a leather needle and the foot to a walking foot. Change the thread if desired. Take the corresponding leather panel, tape it in position *right side up* with the edge over the line you just stitched, opposite the lining, and stitch in place. Remember to reverse stitch at the start and end of the line to secure the stitching (b).

4. Repeat Steps 2 and 3 on the other side of the zipper starting with the lining (c). Remember to change presser feet and needles over each time (d).

5. Your zipper is now secured in place. Cut away any loose threads and remove any tape (if used) from the back of the lining fabric and leather (e).

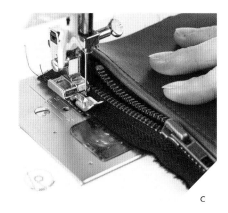

c

ZIPPER ENDS

Cover your zipper ends for a neat finish, with matching or contrasting leather.

1. Cut two squares of leather twice the width of your zipper. Apply glue to the *wrong side* of the leather then fold in half to encase the zipper ends (cover the fabric only, don't touch the metal). Sew across the edge of the leather to secure (f).

2. Insert the zipper as usual, sewing the leather ends into the seam allowance.

Folded leather is quite thick, so ease the work through the machine carefully to ensure the needle and thread do not break.

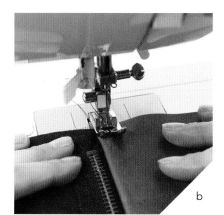

a

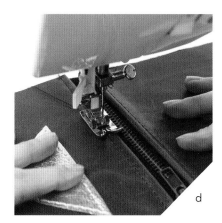

d

b

e

f

SURFACE TREATMENTS

To finish your work, you can burnish the edges or polish the surface. This only applies to vegetable-tanned leather as it works with the natural oils retained in the fibres (these oils are removed during chrome dyeing).

BURNISHING

Friction melts the leather fibres which the tool then burnishes smooth. The beeswax adds the necessary slip and finish.

1. Rub the edge of your finished project a few times with a piece of beeswax (a).

2. Take a burnisher (or a smooth cloth), and run it up and down the edge as shown. This helps the leather absorb the wax, and polishes and rounds the edge at the same time (b).

POLISHING

Apply saddle soap (use on vegetable-tanned leather *only*) using a soft clean sponge or cloth in circular motions. Apply a thin layer, leave to dry for 4–5 hours, then apply again; repeat a third time. Your leather will be slightly darker but also protected from stains and the elements (c).

a

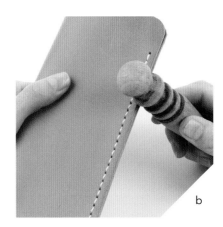

b

c

PAINTING EDGES

This is a subtle but effective way to highlight the edge of your leather and add a pop of colour. It works best on leather that is at least 2mm thick and fairly stiff – usually vegetable-tanned only.

1. The edge to be painted should be free of dust or snags, and free of any beeswax or polish that might have been used elsewhere.

2. Apply the paint using a small detail brush. Take care to keep the paint on the edge of the leather only, keeping it from touching the front or back of the leather. Leave to dry for 10–15 minutes (d).

3. Once the first coat is completely dry, lightly sand it to create a key for the second coat. Rub away specks of dust from sanding using a smooth cloth, then apply the second coat.

4. Repeat this process until you're happy with the finish of the final coat of dried paint (e), then buff with the cloth.

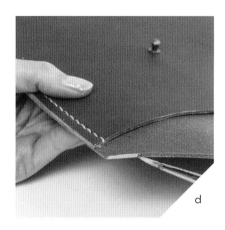
d

a

EMBOSSING

There are numerous letter stamping sets you can buy in different fonts and sizes, varying in price from a few pounds to hundreds! There are pre-made stamps in various patterns, or have your own designs made up fairly inexpensively (*see* Resources).

To emboss using stamps and pressure only, you need to use vegetable-tanned leather as this will hold the shape best. To stamp onto chrome-dyed leather, the leather needs to be fairly thick – at least 2mm – and have the grain removed to create a smooth surface. Otherwise, heat is required for the embossed shapes to be fixed into the leather.

b

STAMPING SEPARATE LETTERS

The most affordable letter sets require only a mallet and hard surface (**a**). However, for writing words it is difficult to get the letters perfectly in line, as you stamp each letter separately.

USING A CHAMBER

You can purchase a letter set with a chamber to secure the letters and emboss them in a perfectly straight line (**b**). Do note that you will need to buy multiple letters and numbers if any words or dates have the same character more than once.

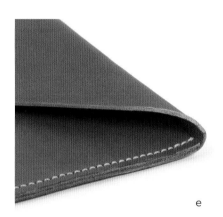
e

Always test out the paint and technique on scrap leather. This allows you to see whether mistakes can be easily cleaned off!

Chambers are available as soldering iron attachments to be used with foil, but results can be inconsistent.

TEMPLATES

Trace or transfer the templates
onto card, enlarging or adapting if
instructed in the project instructions.

KEY

—— Cut outer edge

—— Cut line

- - - Fold line

- - - Masking tape line

◯ Punch hole

HANDY TIPS

· Leather comes in different thicknesses
so you may need to adjust some templates
slightly for the pieces to fit together.

· 'Measure twice, cut once' is very true
with leather – it can be an expensive
material, so take great care when
measuring.

· Hole sizes for projects such as the
Punched Cuff can be adjusted to fit
personal taste.

· A PDF of all the full-sized templates
can be downloaded from
http://ideas.sewandso.co.uk/patterns/

BOLD CUFFS
PUNCHED CUFF

Full size (adjust length
to fit wrist)

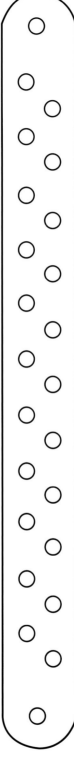

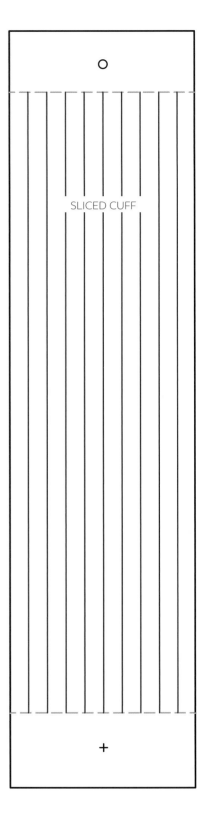

SLICED CUFF

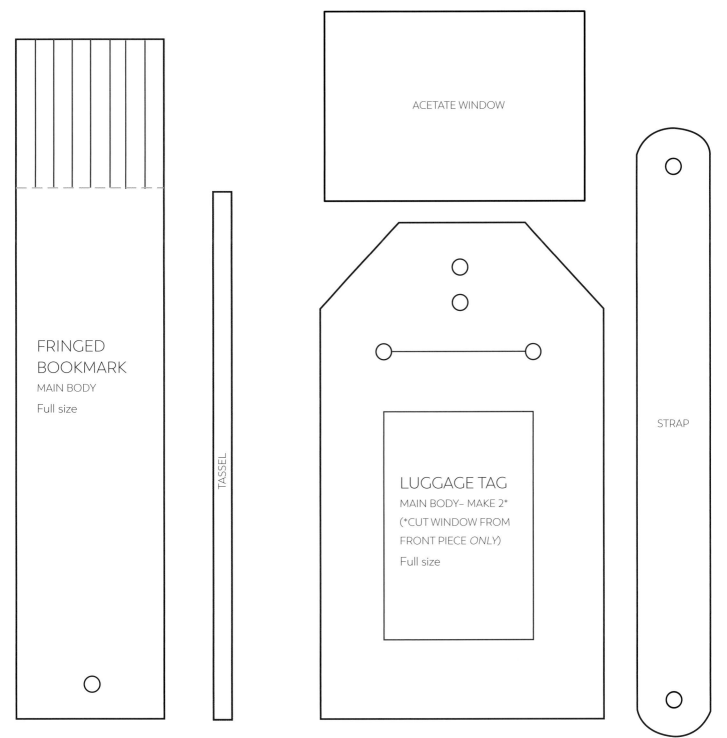

FRINGED
BOOKMARK

MAIN BODY

Full size

TASSEL

ACETATE WINDOW

LUGGAGE TAG

MAIN BODY– MAKE 2*
(*CUT WINDOW FROM
FRONT PIECE *ONLY*)

Full size

STRAP

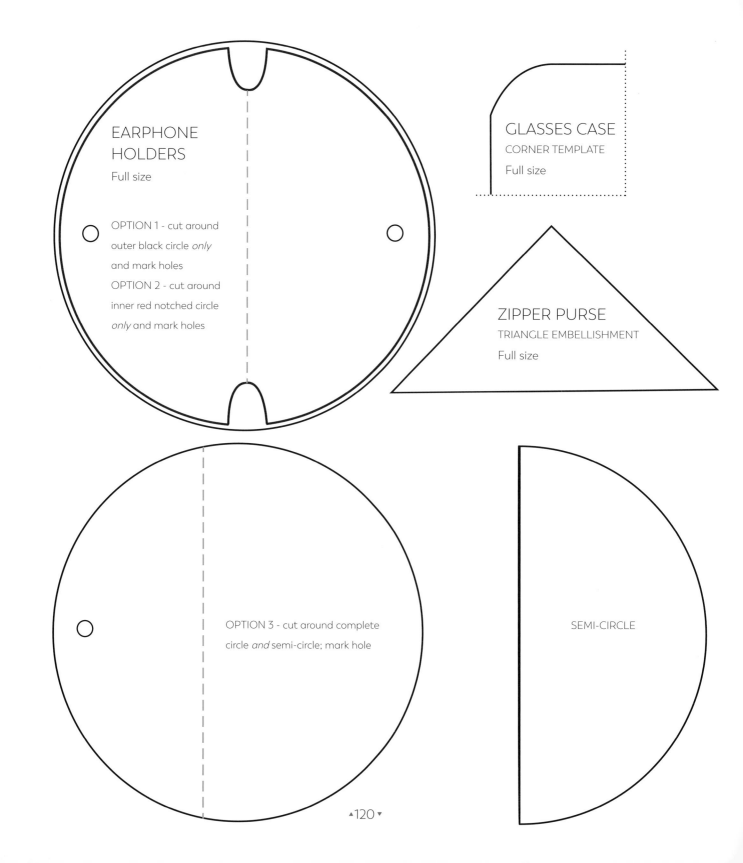

EARPHONE HOLDERS

Full size

OPTION 1 - cut around outer black circle *only* and mark holes

OPTION 2 - cut around inner red notched circle *only* and mark holes

GLASSES CASE

CORNER TEMPLATE

Full size

ZIPPER PURSE

TRIANGLE EMBELLISHMENT

Full size

OPTION 3 - cut around complete circle *and* semi-circle; mark hole

SEMI-CIRCLE

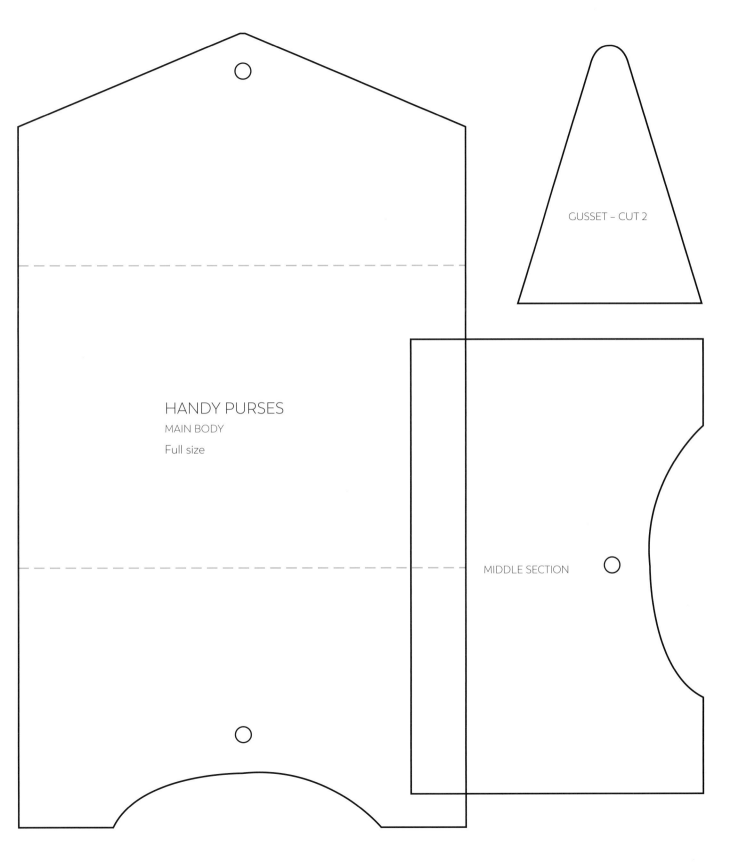

GUSSET – CUT 2

HANDY PURSES

MAIN BODY

Full size

MIDDLE SECTION

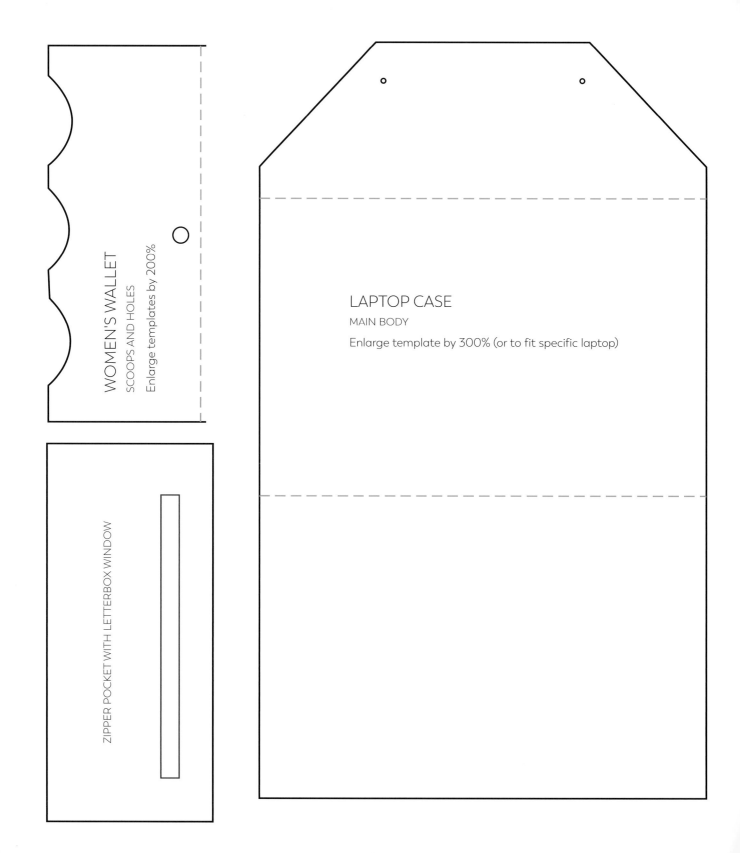

WOMEN'S WALLET
SCOOPS AND HOLES
Enlarge templates by 200%

ZIPPER POCKET WITH LETTERBOX WINDOW

LAPTOP CASE

MAIN BODY

Enlarge template by 300% (or to fit specific laptop)

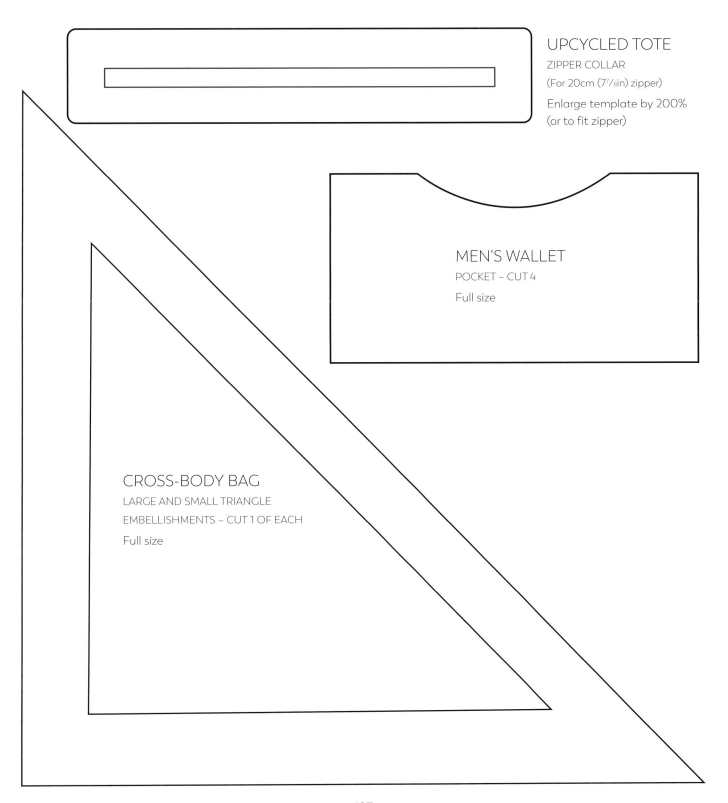

UPCYCLED TOTE
ZIPPER COLLAR
(For 20cm (7⅞in) zipper)
Enlarge template by 200%
(or to fit zipper)

MEN'S WALLET
POCKET – CUT 4
Full size

CROSS-BODY BAG
LARGE AND SMALL TRIANGLE
EMBELLISHMENTS – CUT 1 OF EACH
Full size

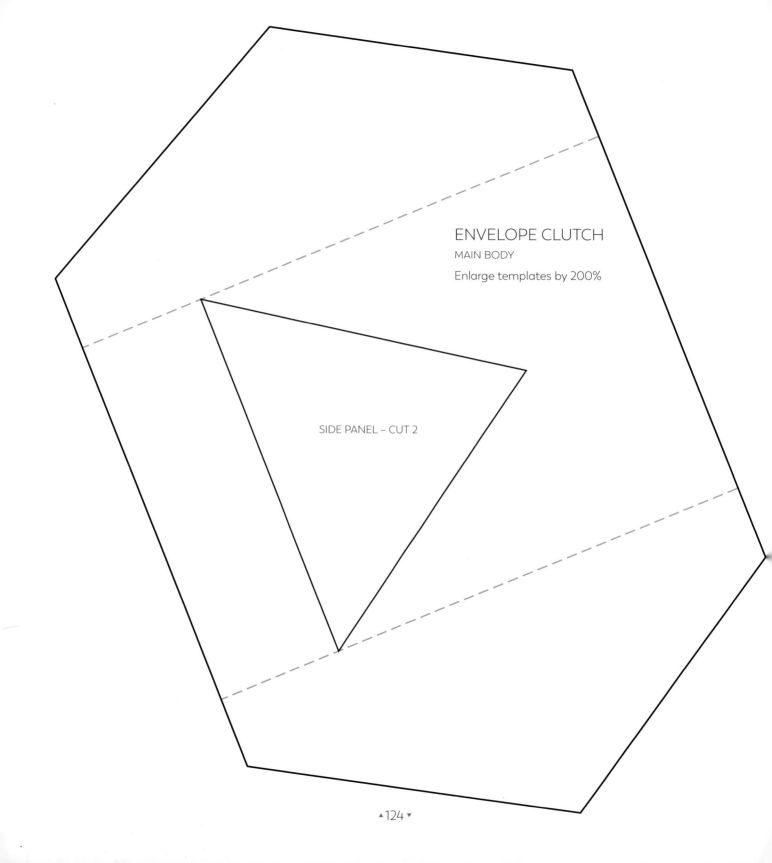

ENVELOPE CLUTCH

MAIN BODY

Enlarge templates by 200%

SIDE PANEL – CUT 2

RESOURCES

COURSES AND FURTHER STUDY

ROSANNA CLARE HANDMADE ACCESSORIES

tel: 07979 782491
email: info@rosannaclare.com
www.rosannaclare.com
Rosanna runs a number of short courses from her Surrey studio including making leather accessories and handbags, and upcycling jackets into bags

LEATHER

BLENKINSOP LEATHERS LTD

Newton Road, Higham Ferrers, Northamptonshire NN10 8HW
tel: 01933 317377
email: blenkinsopleathers@tiscali.co.uk
www.blenkinsopleathers.com
Bespoke colour matching service

JT BATCHELOR LTD

9–10 Culford Mews, London, N1 4DZ
tel: 020 7254 2962
email: info@jtbatchelor.co.uk
www.jtbatchelor.co.uk
Tools, dyes and vegetable-tanned hides

WALTER REGINALD

Unit 6, 100 The Highway, London E1W 2BX
tel: 020 7481 2233
email: info@walterreginald.com
www.walterreginald.co.uk
Large warehouse of expensive but good quality leather, tools and equipment

ALMA LTD

Block D, 12–14 Greatorex St, London E1 5NF
tel: 020 7377 0762
email: info@alma1938.com
www.alma1938.com
Selection of chrome-dyed and vegetable-tanned leathers. Offcuts in a variety of finishes for starting out and small projects

OTHER MATERIALS

LONDON TRIMMINGS

26–28 Cambridge Heath Road, Whitechapel, London E1 5QH / 41B Antill Road, Tottenham Hale, London N15 4AS
tel: 0207 790 2233
email: enquiries@londontrimmings.co.uk
www.londontrimmings.co.uk
Hardware, fastenings, threads and more

S&K FITTINGS

Unit 0GF, Leroy House, 436 Essex Road, London N1 3QP
tel: 020 7354 4435
email: info@skfittings.co.uk
www.skfittings.co.uk
Metal fittings, interfacing, threads, zippers

GREEN GRIZZLY (HEBAR-LTD ON EBAY)

Unit D2, Spectrum Business Centre, Anthony's Way, Rochester, Kent ME2 4NP
tel: 07463 114104
contact form: www.greengrizzly.co.uk/en/contact-us
www.greengrizzly.co.uk
Great for fastenings, bag hardware and related haberdashery

OTHER SUPPLIES & EQUIPMENT

WILLIAM GEE

520–522 Kingsland Road, London, E8 4AH
tel: 020 7254 2451
email: info@williamgee.co.uk
www.williamgee.co.uk
Wholesaler of fabrics and trimmings

WIMBLEDON SEWING CO LTD

292–312 Balham High Rd, London SW17 7RF
tel: 020 8767 4724
email: wimbledonsewingmachinecoltd@btinternet.com
Supplier of new and refurbished domestic and industrial sewing machines including Bernina, Janome, Brother, Elna. In-house servicing, spares and repairs

SEWING & CRAFT SUPERSTORE

292–312 Balham High Rd, London SW17 7RF
tel: 020 8767 0036
email: sewingandcraftsuperstore@btinternet.com
www.craftysewer.com
Massive store with fabric, haberdashery, fabric dye, machines, some leather offcuts and more

ONLINE ONLY

ARTISAN LEATHER

www.artisanleather.co.uk
Leather craft supplies website selling leather, tools, hardware, glue and more

DIAMOND AWL

tel: 07889 097516
email: jason@diamondawl.co.uk
www.diamondawl.co.uk
Workshops, tools, and kits for beginners

ABOUT THE AUTHOR

Rosanna Gethin's leatherwork skills have been mainly self-taught over the years and having a creative family (a painter and picture framer for a mother and carpenter for a father) means that making is in her blood; it was inevitable that she would also end up in a creative career. Rosanna discovered her love for leather 15 years ago, while browsing Spitalfields Market. As a recent graduate with a Graphic Design degree, she immediately looked for ways to create her own leather bags on a budget. After buying two pieces of leather and taking a sewing lesson from mum, Rosanna never looked back. As a Design Technology Teacher she introduced bag making to her GCSE class, and honed her technique and teaching skills. With a Masters Degree, Rosanna set up her own full-time business making leather bags and accessories, teaching workshops and now writing books! Rosanna lives in Surrey with her partner Luke and dog Izza. She recently moved into a new studio in the countryside, which is large, light and has a big new work bench (made by her crafty father of course!) on which to run workshops and to continue to design and make. As well as her passion for leather Rosanna also enjoys pottery, running, cycling and skiing.

ACKNOWLEDGMENTS

I would like to thank everyone at F&W not only for all their hard work and patience with me on the making of this book, but also for approaching me in the first place! I feel very proud to be the author of my very own leather craft book and couldn't have done it without them.

Also, my family for all their support and belief in me, as well as their feedback on various parts of the book, not to mention my good friend and very talented designer Nancy Leschnikoff for her invaluable advice and expertise as a book designer herself.

INDEX

A SEWANDSO BOOK

© F&W Media International, Ltd 2018

SewandSo is an imprint of F&W Media International, Ltd
Pynes Hill Court, Pynes Hill, Exeter, EX2 5AZ, UK

F&W Media International, Ltd is a subsidiary of F+W Media, Inc
10151 Carver Road, Suite #200, Blue Ash, OH 45242, USA

Text and Designs © Rosanna Gethin 2018
Layout and Photography © F&W Media International, Ltd 2018

First published in the UK and USA in 2018

A catalogue record for this book is available from the British Library.

ISBN-13: 978-1-4463-0676-5 paperback
SRN: R6808 paperback

ISBN-13: 978-1-4463-7649-2 PDF
SRN: R7611 PDF

ISBN-13: 978-1-4463-7650-8 EPUB
SRN: R7610 EPUB

Printed in China by RR Donnelley for:
F&W Media International, Ltd
Pynes Hill Court, Pynes Hill, Exeter, EX2 5AZ, UK

10 9 8 7 6 5 4 3 2 1

Content Director: Ame Verso
Acquisitions Editor: Sarah Callard
Managing Editor: Jeni Hennah
Project Editor: Jenny Fox-Proverbs
Design Manager: Lorraine Inglis
Designer: Ali Stark
Photographer: Jason Jenkins
Production Manager: Beverley Richardson

31901063603098

F&W Media publishes high quality books on a wide range of subjects.
For more great book ideas visit: www.sewandso.co.uk

Layout of the digital edition of this book may vary depending on reader hardware and display settings.